DON'T DROP *your* SALVATION

DON'T DROP *your* SALVATION

Lay Hold on Eternal Life
1 Timothy 6:19

PROFESSOR KOFI A. AMOATENG

Library of Congress Control Number: 2022909540

HARDBACK: 978-1-957575-63-6
PAPERBACK: 978-1-957575-62-9
EBOOK: 978-1-957575-64-3

Ordering Information:

For orders and inquiries, please contact:
1-888-404-1388
www.goldtouchpress.com
book.orders@goldtouchpress.com

Printed in the United States of America

Contents

Acknowledgments vii

Executive Summary ix

Chapter 1: Busted Salvation... 1

Chapter 2: The Lost in the Lost Church........................44

Chapter 3: Do not compromise your faith & Salvation... 71

Chapter 4: You must be born again to keep your
             ticket to Heaven 98

Chapter 5: Trading Heaven for Hell 126

Chapter 6: Positive Tongue saves.................................. 148

Chapter 7: Tattoo Mania: Are they cool for Christians? 168

Chapter 8: Invest in the Kingdom of God. 195

Acknowledgments

First and foremost, I would like to thank God. I am thankful for every day and the gift of writing. Writing is about the joy of creating and broadcasting your passion to all the corners of the World. My passion is the Word of God. In the process of putting this book together, I realized how true this gift of writing is for me. God has given me the keys to unlock puzzles in the Scriptures. Father, you have given me the power to believe in my passion and pursue my dream of writing like the Apostle Paul. I could never have done this without the faith I have in You, the Almighty God. The Lord saved me from bondage, and to keep my salvation, I have to obey him forever and also save many souls for him. My sincere gratitude goes to my Lord and personal Savior, Jesus Christ of Nazareth, who has three times saved me from death in 1995, 2010, and 2019, respectively. I am sold out to you forever. Words are weak to describe your protection, counsel, teaching, instructions, and directions for my life and my third book. I love you more than I would ever be able to express. I love you to death.

My second and deepest appreciation goes to one of my daughters, Ivana, who suddenly got a mental illness that is yet to be healed by the Lord Jesus Christ. She ended down in Ghana, where she continues to suffer untold hardships from family members and strangers who took care of her in the most trying times of her life. During her ordeal, I met all kinds of false prophets and pastors who cleverly took thousands of dollars from me without being able to help her. The majority of those who claim to know our Lord God are false. ***"They profess that they know God: but in works they deny him, being abominable, and disobedient, and unto every good work reprobate" (Titus 1:16).*** Don't be fooled by their cooked-out miracles and signs.

I draw strength from your illness to write and dive into the spiritual realms. Your illness is my own Job's travail. Aside from the Lord Jesus, your illness kept the Holy Ghost's fire in me so I could complete my third spiritual book,

Her illness and my own daily cross made me understand the Psalmist ***"For the rod of the wicked shall not rest upon the lot of the righteous; lest the righteous put forth their hands unto iniquity" (Psalm 125:3).***

Executive Summary

A little over two years since volume 2 of Watch and Pray was published, wickedness and lies have overwhelmed our world. In the midst of all these, the wise are thirsty and hungry for the unadulterated word of God as prophet Amos admonished us. ***"Behold, the days come, saith the Lord God, that I will send a famine in the land, not a famine of bread, nor a thirst for water, but of hearing the words of the Lord. And they shall wander from sea to sea, and from the north even to the east, they shall run to and fro to seek the word of the Lord, and shall not find it" (Amos 8:11-12).*** Lord, help us to hang onto our salvation because deception is deepening, lies have supplanted the truth, the wicked continue to do wickedly, and false prophets and pastors continue to spread false prophecies and fake healings. Things are continually and desperately falling apart, and COVID-19 Pandemic lingers on. In all these situations, there are few Christians who are fed up with falsehood, lies, and deception and are thirsty and hungry for the unadulterated word of God.

The new volume of ***Don't Drop your Salvation,*** lays out how to work out your own salvation with fear and trembling ***(Philippians 2:12b).*** It contains the keys to lock your eternal salvation. Furthermore, it connects all the dots on working out our salvation with fear and trembling by dying to self, loving others for Jesus Christ's sake, and obeying God forever. The second coming of the Lord is drawing closer, so this book has many topics that will convict and convert many souls to hold onto their salvation. This book is your ticket to heaven. The abstracts are only scoops of what this book contains.

The layout of the book is as follows:

1. **Busted Salvation:**
   HEAVEN and hell discussions do not sit well with even the so-called born-again Christians because many of them are in delusion. Many live as if after this life, there is nothing else. Beloved, whether you believe it or not, after this life we are living, we will enter into eternity. We will spend eternity in either heaven or hell. The question is, where will you spend eternity? In hell or heaven? It is the hard truth that if you reject Christ, you will go to hell. Who is going to hell? The almost persuaded such as King Agrippa and many who were close to accepting the gospel of Christ will be lost eternally. With pain and anguish, they will weep and gnash their teeth when they are led away from Heaven's gate. Many Christians have been in churches forever and still do not have a relationship with God. They profess they know Him, but God does not know them. Moreover, the profession of faith alone is not enough for your salvation. You must be a true born-again Christian. The eternal regret of being almost persuaded will be devastating. Why are many believers becoming almost persuaded and end up losing their salvation? They will miss eternal salvation by a narrow margin because

they do not work out their own salvation with fear and trembling by not putting others ahead of themselves and disobeying God.

2. **The Lost in the Lost Church:**
The church has lost its neutrality in the pursuit of the truth. The church is facing much more moral crisis than ever. Truth is taken as lies, while lies have become the truth. Lies become the truth if the church and Christians allow them. There is more opposition to telling the truth than lies. Chaos is gradually increasing in our churches, and God's judgment is eminent. The church is full of disinformation and misinformation on the word of God. Judgment is awaiting us and many of us who feel saved. We are going to have a rude awakening when the Lord's trumpet sounds. There will be weeping and gnashing of teeth because many of us who feel heaven-bound would be surprised to find ourselves with the wicked in hell. Most of the weeping and gnashing of teeth would come from the so-called Christians who might think they made it to heaven. They are fooling themselves on earth because they have created their own righteousness and holiness outside the Lord's. They are still chilling out with false prophets and teachers who prophesy and teach them lies (Jeremiah 23: 1-2). The church is sleeping and in the doldrums because Great Revivals are not bringing in holy convictions. As the church continues to witness trials, tribulations, and hard times, only those who are marked and moved by the power and glory of God will be the ones who will stand and speak with thunder and with great power. The holiness and righteousness of Jesus is taken as

a joke and mocks God. Meanwhile, agents of Satan are found in every living church. Their job is simply to hinder the spread of the gospel in order to weaken the Church of the Lord. Today, churches are mixed bags of multitude of people. All kinds of people —good and bad, evil and blessed, wicked and godly— go to church, including Satan himself (Exodus 12:38).

3. **Don't Compromise your salvation:**
Do not compromise on anything because small compromises lead to big ones. One small compromise by King David led him to big compromises (2 Samuel 11). The long-term cost of compromising is far greater than non-compromising. Stand up for the truth, despite all odds. Buy-in for the cross and the blood of Jesus and do not sell them out. There is a time to refuse to bow when God's truth directs us to conflict with the prevailing culture around us. When we refuse to bow as in the case of Daniel and his three Hebrew friends, we have to be prepared to get burned. If you do not have the hard experiences of the apostles, particularly Paul, Peter, and Jesus Christ Himself, the probability of you compromising the truth of God is very high. John, the Baptist, was beheaded during Jesus Christ's ministry on earth. Many confessed Christians will chicken out (compromise) when the martyrdom of Jesus Christ is on the line. We need to get the word of God in our system, particularly what Paul taught us in the book of Romans 8: 35-39.

4. You must be born-again:
Why are few Christians experiencing abundant and fruitful life? Many Christians are carnal because they go to church, but Jesus Christ is not their Lord and personal savior. Most Christians waver or vacillate between carnality and spirituality. To be born again is to be saved eternally. Born-again, a true BA degree candidates, experience spiritual transformation Today, many Christians like Nicodemus struggle to understand the meaning of "Born again". Jesus is still telling us that no one enters the kingdom of God without a true BA degree. Nobody can save himself or herself by good works because flesh can only give birth to flesh, but Spirit gives birth to spirit. Everybody needs a change of heart which is the work of the Holy Spirit by God, the death of Christ on the cross (cleansing away our past, present, and future sins), and the resurrection of Jesus Christ (Jesus is still alive and lives forever). The Holy Spirit gives new birth, and he moves like the wind. Nobody controls what the wind does and predicts where the wind goes. Again, nobody can give himself or herself new birth, and everything you give birth to is yourself. It is only God who can bring the change that needs to happen in your life through Jesus Christ. It is indeed the Spirit that gives birth to Spirit. The new birth is purely the work of the Holy Spirit. Like Nicodemus, many Christians are caught up between carnality and spirituality (wavering in their walk with God). They are not born again because they are neither cold nor hot. By my conservative estimate, about 98.0 percent of Christians vacillate between carnality and spirituality.

5. **Trading Heaven for Hell:**
The Christian race is a daily commitment with the Lord. We do not rest on our oars because we stand to lose our salvation as quickly as we receive it. Lot's wife lost her salvation momentarily by looking back at Sodom and Gomorrah. She could not get Sodom and Gomorrah off her mind and slipped to the devil's side. Millions of Christians are trading Heaven for Hell by getting hooked to all the lust, flesh, and pride of this world which are passing away quickly. As I write this chapter, I am wondering how many believers and unbelievers are being deceived by men and women to engage in improper sexual practices that can lead to their ultimate spiritual and physical deaths. Sex, the oldest and the most effective trick of the devil that has taken millions to hell, is the least talked about topic in the ministry of Christ. Many pastors, saints, and other workmen of God feel very uneasy at the mention of sex, but these have fallen victims to it. Why has the enemy used sex as bait to woo many to hell? Why should we cheat, kill and even destroy to gain riches and wealth for a moment and quickly fall into hell forever? Instant gratification (quick pleasures of life) such as money, drugs, sex, and the rest is taking millions to hell. There is hope in waiting on God.

6. **Positive Tongue saves:**
Generally, communication with each other can either make or unmake a relationship. What you say and how it is said can make a whole lot of difference. Christians, in particular, struggle in their daily conversations. Even though we know that Scriptures have much to tell us

about how we are —and are not to use our words, this is still an immense problem, causing headaches and strain not only in family relationships, but also in friendships, work, and church settings. Our speech is either controlled by God or Satan. When God can speak through us, He tells us what to say, how to say, and when to say it. You cannot expect God to use your tongue when you preach ten percent of the gospel and allow the devil to use your tongue for ninety percent. Many people and workmen of God follow this model and have destroyed their ministries by the careless use of their tongues. Therefore, either life can come forth from your tongue, or you can kill people or yourself (physically and spiritually) with it *(Proverbs 18:21)*. Who owns your tongue today? God or Satan? Let God control your tongue through what you get in your heart. To control our tongue, we must first control our hearts. Jesus said that the mouth speaks out that which fills the heart. We should never speak (or write) if we sense a disturbance in our hearts— we need the peace of God to be a referee or an umpire in our hearts. All believers should stop negative talk. We are created to talk and see positively. However, Satan has been pushing negative and conflicting messages in our minds since the fall of man. Stop talking about your feelings, wants, frustrations, and focus on your future in Christ Jesus. You must talk about things that will increase the Lord and decrease you. Do not speak from your heart because above all things, it is desperately wicked. Do not trust your heart, especially when you are angry.

7. Tattoo Mania: Are they cool for Christians?

Today, tattoos have become an immensely popular fashion statement among the youth. People regard tattoo as a way of asserting one's personality and a marker of their identity. Exposure to Western culture has transformed youth immensely as love for tattoos has taken hold. Tattoos have also become influenced by international music stars and sports heroes who often display elaborate body art. The tattoo was until recently reserved for the heavy metal rocker or biker, criminal, the social outcast of society. But today, tattoo glamorously appears everywhere and anywhere. It is the latest fashion craze. Simply, tattoos come from hell. It is a scheme of Satan to destroy and take you to hell. Even one small tattoo is still a tattoo. It does not matter what type of tattoo it is. Even if it is of a cross of Jesus— a tattoo is a tattoo. Satan will mark you for hell if you disobey the Word of God. The Bible says in Leviticus 19:28. Ye shall not make any cuttings in your flesh for the dead, not print or make any marks upon you: I am the Lord." You do not need a tattoo to give you a mark of bravery. It is the Holy Spirit's baptism that gives you power and authority. The trademarks of Christians are the blood of the Lamb in the form of invisible lights in front and behind true Christians, which are sanctified by the Holy Spirit. Christians receive invisible tattoos initiated to them by the Lord Jesus Christ through the Holy Spirit's power. Our names are tattooed on the Lord's hands and in his blood. They are invisible tattoos. You cannot see them with your naked eyes. We cannot defy our bodies with tattoos because they are the temples of

God. When the Holy Spirit's fire is upon you, you will be filled with new wine, and Satan, his demons, and the children of disobedience will be afraid of you. Tattooed folks are cowards because they use physical markings on their bodies as signs of valor. The righteous are as bold as a lion.

8. Invest in the Kingdom of God.

Today, believers and unbelievers are craving for riches in the form of houses, cars, stocks, bonds, real estate, mutual funds, and many more in a hurry. When is the scramble for worldly riches going to reduce, even after COVID-19? It is not going to stop, but it will rather accelerate as we quickly approach End times. If worldly riches are temporal, why are smart people working hard all the time to accumulate wealth upon wealth? Many rich people spend less or no time for God because they are preoccupied with the riches and the habits of the rich. Wealth becomes their god, so they worship it. Listen to the conversation between Jesus and the young ruler in Luke Chapter 18. Jesus and his disciples lived off of the financial generosity of those who had accumulated some wealth. We can use some of the money and all kinds of wealth to get through life and provide for our families, but the lesson is that, don't see these things for more than they are. Don't build your life around these things because most people get consumed by them. The focus of their lives is about accumulating cars, homes, collections, and all forms of investments, but they are all going to perish. Jesus is warning us against the improper values that we place on these treasures. It is through that which so ties us to the world that we risk losing eternal life. It is our affection for these things that give treasures undue values. The choices we make today may result in eternal treasures in heaven. God owns everything we have. We have to trust him in all we undertake. If we do not invest in His kingdom, He can take everything away from us. We do not have to listen and look to the world but be content with what we have. We do not have to get greedy in whatever enterprise we undertake. Do not let money and material possessions compromise your Christian faith. It cost John the Baptist his life when he invested in the kingdom of God by preaching repentance. It also cost Jesus Christ his life when he established the spiritual church in the kingdom of God by preaching the good news. Similarly, it cost all the apostles their lives by crucifixion and related deaths by torture. What is your cost of being a Christian?

Each chapter is unique (in terms of substance and length) and offers you different insights, but all drive you to the salvation gate by connecting you to the Lord of mercy and love.

Chapter 1
Busted Salvation

"And Samuel said, Hath the Lord as great delight in burnt offerings and sacrifices, as in obeying the voice of the Lord? Behold, to obey is better than sacrifice, and to hearken than the fat of rams"

1 Samuel 15:22

"Wherefore the Lord said, for as much as this people draw near me with their mouth, and with their lips do honor me, but have removed their heart far from me, and their fear toward me is taught by the precept of men"

Isaiah 29:13

"Truly in vain is salvation hoped for from the hills, and from the multitude of mountains: truly in the Lord our God is the salvation of Israel"

Jeremiah 3:23

"Not everyone that saith unto me, "Lord, Lord, shall enter into the kingdom of heaven; but he that doeth the will of the Father which is in heaven. Many will say to me in that day, Lord, Lord, have we not prophesied in thy name? And in thy name have cast out devils and in thy name done many wonderful works? And then will I profess unto them, I never knew you; depart from me, ye that work iniquity"

Matthew 7:21-23

"Wherefore, my beloved, as ye have always obeyed, not as in my presence only, but now much more in my absence, work out your own salvation with fear and trembling"

Philippians 2:12

"And this is the will of him that sent me, that everyone which seeth the Son, and believeth on him, may have everlasting life: and I will raise him up at the last day:

John 6:40

"There shall be weeping and gnashing of teeth, when ye shall see Abraham, and Isaac, and Jacob, and all the prophets, in the kingdom of God, and you yourselves thrust out"

Luke 13:28

"And being made perfect, he became the author of eternal salvation unto all them that obey him"

Hebrews 5:9

1. Introduction:

HEAVEN and HELL discussions do not sit well with even the so-called born-again Christians because many of them are in delusion. As it is appointed unto men once to die but after this judgment *(Hebrews 9:27)*. Many live as if after this life, there is nothing else. Beloved, whether you believe it or not, after this life we are living, we will enter into eternity. We will spend eternity in either heaven or hell. The question is, where will you spend eternity? In hell or heaven? It is the hard truth that if you reject Christ, you will go to hell. Who is going to hell? The almost persuaded, such as King Agrippa and many who were close to accepting the gospel of Christ will be lost eternally. With pain and anguish, they will weep and gnash their teeth when they are led away from Heaven gate. The eternal regret of being almost persuaded by this group will be devastating. They came too close to accepting Christ, but they hardened their hearts.

The most troubling verses in the book of Matthew are in Chapter 7: 21-23. Many in the body of Christ will be faced with this judgment. Who are these Christians? They include many doing what is right in people's eyes. They may be anointed with Spiritual gifts of prophecies or words of knowledge but denied Heaven entrance. Many have cast wicked spirits from many sick people. Others have built mega-churches, fed the poor, supplied relief funds for the hungry in poor nations. Others have organized large crusades and delivered the sick and got many saved, but they stepped out of eternity. Hard-working workmen of God such as Sunday school teachers, pastors, evangelists, song composers, musicians, choir members, elders, Deacons, Deaconesses, and many more run the risk of being rejected entrance to the kingdom of Heaven. Even many with ministries, judged by large crowds as elites in God's army stand the risk of losing eternity (fall into a spiritual wasteland). Who else can be saved?

The body of Christ must avoid hell by examining every aspect of their lives, ministries, and their daily walk with God and assessing if they are in alignment with God's plan and purpose in their lives. The elect of God with a saving relationship with God will by all means make it to Heaven, even if they detour to the devil's side somewhere in their life cycles.

> ***"Moreover whom he did predestinate, them he also called: and whom he called, he justified: and whom he justified, them he also glorified. Who shall lay anything to the charge of God's elect? It is God that justified"***
>
> ***Romans 8:30, 33***

The elect is chosen by God before birth and enjoys an intimate and saving relationship with God ***(Matthew 24: 21-22).*** The elect includes God's own people such as prophets, pastors, teachers, elders, Deacons, Deaconesses, and ordinary

Christians who constantly have intimacy with God and live in holiness and righteousness of God.

Another group of people who will get a pass at the Heaven entrance will be the flock of sheep in obedience, holiness, and righteousness of God. The Lord protects, feeds, and guides the living water. It is the daily one-on-one relationship with Jesus Christ that matters and not the intermediary relationship with your prophets and pastors. These people who follow Jesus Christ as sheep follow their shepherd will not be denied Heaven entrance. They daily seek the truth from the scriptures and find their way to him. John gospel lays it out here:

> ***"My sheep hear my voice, and I know them, and they follow me. That the saying might be fulfilled, which he spake, of them, which thou gavest me have I lost none."***
>
> ***John 10:27 and John 18:9***

Following Jesus Christ in holiness and righteousness of God leads to Heaven but following false teachers and pastors who are wolves in sheep clothing, fleecing the body of Christ will take you directly to hell.

Finally, there will be at least four surprises on the judgment day: They are (a) Those who from outward appearances (human judgment) should not make it at the heaven gate, made it by God's grace and saving relationship (The elect sake). The Lord will accept them in eternity and tell them this. "Well done, thou good and faithful servant: thou good and faithful over a few things, I will make thee ruler over many things:

enter thou into the joy of the Lord" *(Matthew 25:21)*, (b) Those who from human judgment should easily make it at the heaven gate, because of their works such as healing, casting of demons, positions in their churches, kindness to the poor and many more, are denied eternity. These people will weep and gnash their teeth in anger and anguish for missing heaven. The Lord seeth not as man seeth: for man looketh on the outward appearance, but the Lord looketh on the heart *(1 Samuel 16:7)*, (c) some friends and family members such as fathers, mothers, brothers, sisters, sons, daughters, cousins, nephews, nieces, and grandchildren will be separated and lost eternally, and (d) some friends and family members such as fathers, mothers, brothers, sisters, sons, daughters, cousins, nephews, nieces, and grandchildren will make it at heaven gate.

Therefore, I charge all my readers to pursue their salvation with fear and trembling as Apostle Paul suggested to the Church in Philippi *(Philippians 2:12).* This is what Apostle Paul called salvation paradox *"We must work, and God works"*.

Salvation is the cornerstone of the Christian faith, but it is the most misunderstood subject in Christian circles. It is the least talked-about topic and vaguely discussed because it brings chills to even pastors and preachers. It is the most important subject in the Church, but it is the most confusing and poorly discussed subject. Furthermore, many Christians have come up with different interpretations to satisfy their own selfish desires. Indeed, there is not even a close second among all the many topics that have been preached over the centuries. Salvation is the greatest spiritual miracle to a believer after death or rapture, whichever comes first.

2. The Elect and Eternity

Salvation was a gift of grace given to Christians and God knew before the creation of the world and is predestined (the very elect) *(Romans 8:29-30)*. However, it is not a free pass to the very elect. God's elects are more likely to repent and believe the word of God than children of disobedience. For those God foreknew, He also predestined to be conformed to the likeness of his Son, that he might be the firstborn among many brothers. And those he predestined, he also called; those he called, he also justified, those he justified, he also glorified. God foreknew some people in a saving relationship. God knows many of us in an intimate saving relationship (the elect and others). God knew Jeremiah and many more in their mothers' wombs before they were born (Jeremiah 1:5). He knew Jeremiah, Isaiah, Moses, Abraham, Elijah, and many more in saving relationships. He selected them not based on merits of their own but based on grace (unmerited favor). God knows everybody on the planet and selects us by grace. He is loving and fair in all His ways and listens to what Paul said about God in the book of Romans.

> *"As it is written, Jacob have I loved, Esau have I hated"*

> *Romans 9:13*

The Lord knew many elects before birth and does not know many popes, bishops, archbishops, prophets, evangelists, pastors, elders, Deacons, Deaconesses, and ordinary churchgoers. Why? The Lord knows it all (He is omniscient) and knows the nature of the intimate relationship, holy lifestyles, and righteousness of these people. If the Lord does not know you, then you are out of God's will, and you will ultimately lose eternity

Furthermore, they will live holy lives even under perseverance for the rest of their Christian journeys on earth. The elect of God may be sinners like you and me, chosen by God from eternity past to be saved. They might have been detoured in their Christian lives (living in unrighteousness and un-holiness), but they will make it at the Heaven gate. Jesus spoke about the eternal covenant of redemption in Chapter 17 of John's gospel for the elect.

> ***"I have manifested thy name unto the men which thou gavest me out of the world: thine they were, and but the thou hast given me are of thee. For I have given unto them the words which thou gavest me; and they have received them, and have known surely that I came out from thee, and they have believed that thou elect of God and the children of are thine. And all mine are thine, and thine are mine; and I am glorified in them"***

> ***John 17:6-10***

Daniel clearly distinguishes between the elect of God and the children of disobedience and rebellion.

> ***"And such as do wickedly against the covenant shall he corrupt by flatteries; but the people that***

know their God shall be strong, and do exploits. Many shall be purified and made white and tried, but the wicked shall do wickedly, and none of the wicked shall understand, but the wise shall understand"

Daniel 11:32 and Daniel 12:10.

No matter what the elect of God may go through in life with many detours, they will still make it to heaven:

"For there shall arise false Christs, and false prophets, and shall show great signs and wonders: insomuch that, if it were possible, they shall deceive the very elect"

Matthew24:24

Salvation is not by good works but by grace through the precious blood of Jesus Christ and by true repentance. People everywhere need to get saved and stay saved, but salvation does not come cheap. The Christian life is a war against sin. Sin not only defiles a man but can bring quick spiritual death to the righteous.

Many who miss heaven gate are not careful with their salvation and joke with it.

Salvation is a gift of God validated by the obedience of Jesus Christ.

> **"And being made perfect, he became the author of eternal salvation unto all them that obey him"**
>
> **Hebrews 5:9**

Salvation without making the Lord Jesus Christ your personal savior is hopeless and meaningless. Only Christians who obey Jesus have eternal salvation. When you have Jesus in your life and when you are Holy Spirit-filled, you cannot veer off eternal salvation. Apostle Paul echoes it best in Philippians:

> **"I can do all things through Christ which strengthened me"**
>
> **Philippians 4:13**

Jesus in you gives you victory over sin and many works of the flesh such as arrogance, conceit, crookedness, deceitfulness, evil, greed, insidiousness, cunning, selfishness, ignobility, and more.

What about other religious sects who have no allegiance with Christ? Since Jesus will judge the world, they are all going to miss the salvation mark. What a delusion? What will happen to the Jehovah's Witnesses, Mormons, and Christian Science on the judgment day? The truth is that such people who profess salvation but do not obey Christ have a different faith. Salvation is for Christians who obey Jesus. Many Christians seem oblivious to true salvation because they are still not born-again (they are not children who depend on their parents for nourishment). They include the false prophets, pastors, teachers, elders, and other workmen of God who live in a false sense of salvation.

Salvation is a conditional reality and comes through grace from God, finished work of Christ on the cross, and continuous obedience to the word of God. There is no salvation without Christ, and there is no Christianity without Christ. You cannot work your way to heaven, but if you let Jesus save you by grace, you will make it in the end.

> ***"To whom God would make known what is the riches of the glory of this mystery among the Gentiles; which is Christ in you, the hope of glory: Whom we preach, warning every man, and teaching every man in all wisdom, that we may present every man perfect in Christ Jesus"***
>
> ***Colossians 1: 27-28***

3. ABC of True Salvation [Progress in Sanctification]

What is true salvation, and how do you pursue it throughout the life of a Christian on earth? Salvation is a free gift and the work of God. We are not given salvation certificates the moment we become born-again. It is a work that continues after the Holy Spirit baptism till we are made into the full image of Christ. Generally, the scripture teaches us that we are saved not by our works but by grace through faith in Jesus Christ.

> **"For by grace are ye saved through faith; and that not of yourselves: it is the gift of God. Not of works, lest any man should boast"**
>
> ***Ephesians 2: 8-9***

Salvation is a free gift of God, but it does not come cheap. It goes through a spiritual growth called sanctification. It is a daily transformation into the full image of Christ. Some believers think that the process of salvation happens solely by a work of God without the participation of man. Simply put, what believers should do is "Let go and let God do it" To the grace preachers, it is grace, grace, and grace to the exclusion of any discipline of our own. Why did Paul tell us to exercise ourselves to godliness *(1 Timothy 4:7)*. On the flip side, we have preachers who think salvation is work, work, and work to the exclusion of reliance on God. They rely totally on works of the flesh. Listen to what brother Paul retorted the Galatians who turned to the works of flesh after toiling many years in the Spirit.

> **"O Foolish Galatians, who hath bewitched you, that ye should not obey the truth, before whose eyes Jesus Christ hath been evidently set forth, crucified among you. This only would I learn of you. Received ye the Spirit by the works of the law, or by the hearing of faith? Are ye so foolish? Having begun in the Spirit, are ye now made perfect by the flesh?"**
>
> ***Galatians 3:1-3***

What then is sustainable sanctification? Again, Paul is telling all believers and the church to work out their own salvation with fear and trembling *(Philippians 2: 12-13)*. Paul offers a paradox here. Thus, believers must work, and God works. The process of sanctification is complete when we work alongside God. God works in us to will and does of his good pleasure *(Philippians 2:13)*. The hard truth is that we must work while God is working. God is working, so we must also work to keep our salvation. God works about 99.0 percent with us on our sanctification, and we chip in about 1.0percent of our time and energy. This is why nobody should boast when we get to Heaven because God did it all.

Again, brother Paul inserts himself in the working of God with the man in sanctification below:

> ***"For I am the least of the apostles, that am not meet to be called an apostle, because I persecuted the church of God. By the grace of God, I am what I am: and his grace which was bestowed upon me was not in vain; but I labored more abundantly than they all: yet not I, but the grace of God which was with me"***

> ***1 Corinthians 15: 9-10***

Paul asserts that God's grace works in each of us (even a sinner like him and me) to grow spiritually, but for some, it is without effect. Some believers resist the work of the Holy Spirit, so they lose their salvation *(Acts 7:51)*. We must let go of all our negatives and work with God in the process of sanctification by responding to the promptings of the Holy

Spirit allowing Him to empower us to accomplish His will for our lives.

3a. How Do Believers sanctify themselves?

The primary focus on the process of sanctification (salvation) is Jesus Christ. He is our link pin and role model. Without him, no one can see heaven. Likewise, all Christians try to model our lives along with Jesus Christ's. Jesus Christ, who is both God and the Holy Spirit, came as a poor servant and was obedient unto death. He is the master we have to fix our eyes on, study and emulate if we want to go to heaven. Paul describes the significant role in our pursuit of salvation.

> ***"Looking unto Jesus the author and finisher of our faith, who for the joy that was set before him endured the cross, despising the shame, and is set down at the right hand of the throne of God. For consider him that endured such contradiction of sinners against himself, lest ye be wearied and faint in your minds"***
>
> ***Hebrews 12:2-3***

John's gospel captured Jesus' speech, saying I am the way, the truth, and the life, no man cometh unto the Father, but by me *(John 14:6)*. Salvation is a free gift from God. But to keep it, you must focus and know him. Anyone who has a fixed look on Christ is trying to know and please him in everything he does. In order to grow in our pursuit of sanctification, we must maintain undivided attention to Christ. We are aware of Peter's story in the book of Matthew when he took his eyes off Jesus Christ on the Sea **(Matthew 14:22-23).** The trick of Satan to stop our spiritual growth is to tune us off Jesus and focus on our sins, him and demons, conspiracy theories, the world, and many things that will consume us. We focus on Christ only to get sanctified. Paul's focus was on Jesus and wanted to know him *(Philippians 3:10).* He pressed on to take hold of that for which Christ took hold of him. He was made into Christ's image in the end. Paul was sold out to Christ and embraced His sufferings, death on the cross, and resurrection. In order to be sanctified, like Paul, every believer must focus on Christ.

In order to be sanctified, believers must know the love of God- It was the love of Christ that motivated great apostles like Paul, Peter, and John, and other great men of God to suffer, serve, preach, and even die in the line of duty for Christ. Paul taught the Church of Ephesus to understand the love of Christ *(Ephesians 3:17-19).* He prayed that they are rooted and established in love, may have power, together with all saints, to get to know how wide and long and high and deep is the love of Christ, and must grow in to know this love that surpasses knowledge — that you may be filled to the measure of all the fullness of God. Thus, the love of Christ compels believers to progress in their spiritual growth (working out their salvation). Satan always confuses believers that God does not love us. With Eve, Satan made her doubt the love of God, thereby encouraging her to sin. With Job, Satan made her wife encourage Job to curse God and die. But Job's reply was that "even if God slay me I will still trust him *(Job 13:5).* We grow to know God's love through the love of others, prayers, and spending quiet time with God in obedience. Knowing how much God loves us is a significant move to be sanctified. His kindness draws us to repentance. The chief reason why many Christians get discouraged and stagnant in their pursuit of salvation is that they do not really know Christ's love.

In order to be sanctified, believers must grow in total obedience to God— Believers need to be more obedient to God in the pursuit of their salvation. Obedience to God is not only a necessary reality in sanctification, but it is a proof of salvation. We must do more in obedience than just believing because the demons also believe in God. In order to work out their salvation, Paul cautioned the Philippians to obey God much more *(Philippians 2:12).* The Philippians were not perfect because when they failed, they repented and continued to practice total obedience. Anyone who obeys God's words will be blessed by God because God honors His word *(Numbers 23:19 & Isaiah 55:11).* To the obedient servant of God, He gives them more of the word of God, more peace, more fruits of the Holy Spirit, and many more. Obedience to the word of God is an important element to salvation because it protects believers from stagnation and backward movements in their sanctification journey. Believers who are truly part of the kingdom of God hunger and thirst for righteousness as Christ mentioned in the beatitudes *(Matthew 5:6).* Many believers are still like the biblical Israelites, despite miracles, they continue to disobey and stagnate in the sanctification process. Again, like the biblical Israelites, many believers will be turned away from the heaven gate and rot in hell.

In order to be sanctified, believers must practice continuous discipline— Believers must keep on working their salvation with God to the finish line. Salvation is a free gift from God, but we must be disciplined in order to grow spiritually. Jesus Christ taught us the spirit of discipline by rising up early mornings, afternoons, evenings, and nights to pray in solitary confines every day. He never missed a single day of praying. How many believers can discipline themselves in praying daily? Lack of continuity robs many believers of continuous prayer lifestyles. Satan laughs at undisciplined believers because he knows how to lose their guards. He allows them to pray for a few weeks, months, and years but he ambushes them with his devices to be undisciplined in the end. Sanctification happens through rigorous study of the word of God. Believers must be devoted to the study, memorizing, and the word of God. Peter admonishes believers to crave pure spiritual milk to work out their salvation with fear and trembling. If you consistently read and obey the word of God, it will make you look like Christ. Therefore, all believers must have Christ-like discipline in order to grow up into their salvation. Discipline through rigorous prayers, godly fellowship, and mentorships like that of Paul and Timothy, Peter and Mark, and Jesus and his disciples will help grow your salvation.

In order to be sanctified, believers must develop perseverance— The church is full of believers who have not persevered in the discipline of working out their salvation. One of the seven churches (church in Laodicea) had many lukewarm Christians who were spiritually comfortable and lethargic. Many believers fall away because of discord or moral failure in the church, secular thinking, cults, persecutions, and related reasons. Many believers are falling away, but those who persevere to the end will be saved. Apostle Paul defines the product of perseverance in the book of Romans.

> ***"And not only so, but we glory in tribulations also; knowing that tribulation worketh patience. And patience; experience; and experience, hope"***
>
> ***Romans 5:3-4***

But God gives us encouragement to persevere when we feel like quitting.

In order to be sanctified, believers must develop a healthy fear for God— There must be a fear, reverential awe needed in the believer's heart towards God in order to continue to work out his salvation. When we realize the awesomeness of God, we will not give up intimacy with him for other things. King David was a man who held God in reverential fear. He said this in the book of Psalm *"Taste and see that the Lord is good; blessed is the man who takes refuge in him* **(Psalm 34:8).** Also, the angel of the Lord encamps around those who fear him, and he delivers them. In order to work our salvation, we must fear God's discipline and revere God's word. Paul was a man who lived in reverential fear of God, so he writes, "Our God is a consuming fire" *(Hebrews 12:29).* When a believer truly reverences God, it will be a motivation towards holiness and righteousness.

The secret of the Lord is with them that fear him, and he will show them his covenant **(Psalm 25:14).** The fear of the LORD is the beginning of wisdom, and knowledge of the Holy One is understanding **(Proverbs 9:10).** And unto man he said, Behold, the fear of the Lord, that is wisdom; and to depart from evil is understanding **(Job 28: 28).** There are great benefits in reverential fear of the Lord.

In order to be sanctified, believers must allow God to work in them— God works in believers to will and gives them his desires through the Holy Spirit to be holy and maximize their gifts of power, love, and self-discipline. The Holy Spirit produces in believers' desires to do God's will by convicting them to hate and despise sins through God's word. When the glory of God came upon Isaiah, he realized how ruined and unclean he was **(Isaiah 6:5).** Paul was convicted of righteousness by pressing forward to be like Christ daily (holy aspiration). God works in believers to will by reminding them through the Holy Spirit of the coming judgment. Believers will not be condemned for their sins, but they will be rewarded or lose rewards based on their works **(2 Corinthians 5:9-11).** We (believers) must all appear before the judgment seat of Christ that each one of us may receive what is due him for the things done while in the body, whether good or bad. Paul and the apostles wanted rewards not out of selfish ambition but in order to please God and out of his judgment. Paul reminded us of believers who will be saved by fire, but they will receive no rewards in heaven. Sometimes, as we seek God's will about a future decision or what path we should take, he works in believers to do his will by the presence of peace or by the absence of peace.

Another way God works on our will is simply through the manifestation of God's sovereignty, as in the case of Pharaoh when God hardened his heart. God also gives believers the power to work. We must abide in Christ so that his power can fully manifest in our lives to accomplish his work in order to be sanctified. In summary, we must allow the Spirit of God to work with us by revealing the deep things of God to us. It is the same Holy Spirit that raised Jesus Christ from the grave. Many believers are afraid to walk and work with the Holy Spirit because they live in disobedience. They are no longer children of God.

In order to be sanctified, believers must admit that they are all sinners— For all have sinned and come short of the glory of God **(Romans 3:23).** They are all gone aside they are all together become filthy; there is none that doeth good, no, not one **(Psalm 14:3).** Prophet Isaiah goes on to tell all sinners, including me, that our iniquities have separated us from God. Our sins have hidden God's face from us; that we will not hear him **(Isaiah 59:2).** We do not have to be defensive in accepting that we are all sinners. If we confess our sins, God is merciful to forgive us of our unrighteousness and bring us back to salvation. Eternal separation from God to hell is the consequence of sinning against God. God is so rich in mercy that even when we were dead in sins, he revived and made us sit in heavenly places in Christ Jesus **(Ephesians 2:4-6).**

In order to be sanctified, believers must continuously walk in spirit and truth— God is a Spirit, and they that worship him must worship him in spirit and in truth

[John 4:24 & 2 Corinthians 3:17]. Apostle Paul in the book of Romans admonishes us to walk in spirit to keep the Spirit of God **(Romans 8:9)**. Walk in the Spirit, and ye shall not fulfill the lust of the flesh. The evil products of the flesh that get us to hell are manifest in adultery, fornication, uncleanness, lasciviousness, idolatry, witchcraft, hatred, variance, emulations, wrath, strife, seditions, heresies, envying, murders, drunkenness, revellings, and many more **(Galatians 5:16-19).** Now, if we live in the Spirit, let us also walk in the Spirit **(Galatians 5:25).** We must rely on the Spirit of God who searcheth the deep things of God to help us in the difficult things of life. Many believers are currently throwing themselves to sorcerers, wicked men, false prophets, false pastors and teachers, and wolves in sheep clothing for both deep and shallow things of the world **(1 Corinthians 2: 9-12).**

Instead of walking with the Spirit of God, many believers are seeking help in the wrong places and wrong people and are getting hurt in the end. Many are struggling in their sanctification process because they have completely abandoned the Holy Spirit. Your relationship to the Holy Spirit is critical to your salvation.

> *"But the natural man receiveth not the things of the Spirit of God: for they are foolishness into him: neither can he know them, because they are spiritually discerned"*
>
> *1 Corinthians 2:14*

God is speaking, and has been speaking, and has spoken but how many have heard him? Who receives the deep things of the Spirit of God? It is believers who are spiritually matured and communicated with the Holy Spirit who can hear from the Lord. It is the far-right who is spiritually connected to the Lord. However, if you feel completely blackout and have no communication with the Holy Spirit, you are a natural man, and you are on the far-left. At this point, you may be moving from spirituality to carnality. Therefore, the less spiritual you are, the less you can hear from the Lord. If you cannot hear from the Lord, you will be lost eternally.

In order to be sanctified, believers must practice genuine conviction and repentance— Conviction of sin is God's way of inviting sinners to restore fellowship with Him. Also, the conviction of profound consciousness of the presence and holiness of God. And when he comes, he will convict the world concerning sin and righteousness and judgment **(John 16:8).** To execute judgment on all and to convict all the ungodly of all their deeds of ungodliness that they have committed in such an ungodly way, and of all the harsh things that ungodly sinners have spoken against him **(Jude 1:15).** David was a biblical character who got convicted and repented of his transgressions. For I know my transgressions, and my sin is ever before me. Against you, you only, have I sinned and done what is evil in your sight, so that you may be justified in your words and blameless in your judgment. **(Psalm 51:3-4).** Genuine conviction and repentance of the tax collector (Zachaeus) is a classic bible story.

"And when Jesus came to the place, he looked up, and saw him, and said unto him, Zachaeus, make haste, and come down, for today I must abide at thy house. And Zachaeus stood, and said unto the Lord; Behold, Lord, the half of my goods I give to the poor; and if I have taken anything from any man by false accusation, I restore him fourfold. And Jesus said unto him, This day is salvation come to this house, for so much as he also is a son of Abraham. For the son of man is come to seek and to save that which was lost"

Luke 19:5; 8-10

Zachaeus was an elect of God because he got saved by the Lord Jesus himself. For the Son of man is come to seek and save that which was lost. Zachaeus was a story of genuine repentance because, unlike the young ruler, he was willing to give back all he had taken to the poor. It must be noted that you can be convicted without repentance. The unrepentant are the almost persuaded group who got lost eternally.

4. What is stopping you at Heaven Gate?

(i) Secret sins against God and man

Secret sin is a form of a stronghold in which a believer barricades him or herself with layers and layers of immoral acts against the Lord our God. It is a form of fortress whereby man sins and hides his sins away from everybody, including God. God who beholds even the innermost secret of the heart and who sees our sins clearly, no matter how we cover them, is omniscient. Secret sin can be addictive and cancerous if not dealt with from the beginning. Presumptuous sin, like secret sin, is committed consciously or when we know well that it is sin, yet we commit it anyway. It is a sin committed from man's rash confidence in his own will. It can be a sin when God himself forewarns us either through dreams and visions or through the promptings of the Holy Spirit yet commits it anyway. The classic examples of presumptuous sins were the immoral sexual drives of Samson and David. Both men knew that what they were doing did not sit well with them but did it anyway. It is a sin committed with a design of sinning merely for sinning's sake; it is when we plan and relish our sins. Because of this great danger (presumptuous sin), David unlike modern-day Christians, acknowledged his sin when he was confronted by Prophet Nathan. Presumptuous sin can be committed either in public or private against God's will. When it is committed privately, it becomes a secret sin. Examples of modern-day presumptuous and secret sins that send believers to hell gate are a believer who privately listens to ungodly music (rock, hip-hop, etc.) that does not glorify the Lord or someone who enjoys profane movies full of murders, lies, adultery, fornication, sexual immorality, lust, and the like. The hard truth is that secret sin destroys the relationship between man and God. A man starts to follow the direction of Lucifer and one-third of the angels by sinning and destroying his relationship with God. Ultimately, if man remains stiff-necked, after many rebukes, he will be eternally lost. Secret sin, like the sins listed in Galatians 5:19-21 putting one's head in a lion's mouth. You cannot regulate its jaws: neither can you regulate sin. Once you go into it, you cannot tell when you will be destroyed. One danger of secret sin is that a man cannot commit a little sin in secret, without being by-and-by betrayed into a public sin. Secret sins hurt us more because we sin against God's will whereas open sins are against man. Open sins can be contained but secret sins can be buried deep in our hearts and can be multiplied and long-lasting.

The idea, then, is not the absence of sin (1 John reminds us, after all, that we are deceiving ourselves if we deny our sin), but rather an un-ceased pattern of habitual sin which proceeds neither relinquished nor halted. It speaks of apostasy and paints an image of one who, though he or she has intimately known the truth of the Gospel, fails to surrender at some point.

Secret sin, if not confessed apologetically, can slowly send you to hell.

(ii) Self-righteousness

There is no true righteousness to be earned by self-effort **(Romans 3:23)**. Not even the religious Pharisees who resented the idea of Jesus that all men needed repentance and regarded themselves as righteous and looked with contempt on sinners were righteous before the Almighty God. The Pharisees and many believers were self-righteous. Thus, apart from Jesus Christ, all are in the same position before, separated from him and deserving of death **(Romans 6:23)**. Self-righteousness is seeking to save yourself through works and can also be a certainty that you are morally superior to others.Self-righteousness, a root of <u>Laodiceanism</u>, is the most difficult <u>sin</u> to recognize since it is a matter of attitude rather than action. It is complacency in its worse form because it involves regarding oneself as more virtuous than others despite the reality of a deficient spiritual condition. Ezekiel reports that "Your heart was lifted up because of your beauty; you corrupted your wisdom for the sake of your splendor" **(Ezekiel 28:17).** He became greater and more righteous in his own eyes than his Creator. So also being righteous in our own eyes spiritually exposes our sin to <u>God.</u>

You can acknowledge your sin, feel legitimate remorse for your actions, work towards turning away from sin and cast yourself upon the mercy throne of God.

(iii) Lack of fire and passion for the Kingdom of God

The church is losing the fire of the Holy Spirit. It has more members but fewer Christians, more buildings but less relevance, more mechanisms but less supernatural; more administration but less prayer; more sermons but less power; more flesh but less spirit; and more churches but less impact. They are substituting the fire of God with billboards, flyers displaying their branding, marketing, and strategies. The apostles did not need billboards and flyers because they had the fire of the Holy Spirit burning in their hearts. Billboards and flyers are necessary, but they should be the extension of the Holy Spirit fire. The logo of the church was the fire of the Holy Ghost. On the day of the Pentecost, over 3,000 souls were converted by the power of the Holy Ghost. Now, our traditions and culture have made the word of God of no effect **(Mark 7:13).** Witches and occults are filling and running our churches with songs of Hallelujah and making a mockery and ridiculing God. People walk into the church drunk and walk out drunk; sinners go to church and walk out as sinners, and people go to church as fornicators and walk out as fornicators. Our God is a consuming fire, but their wickedness and ungodliness never get consumed.in the church **(Hebrews 12:29).** The fire of the Holy Ghost purifies sinners for holiness and righteousness and consumes wickedness and ungodliness within sinners. All of us are sinners and have fallen short of the glory of God **(Isaiah 64:6-7).** Lord set our hearts on fire of the Holy Ghost. Nothing is more absolute in God's Church and His Sanctuary than the Fire of Holy Ghost anointing. A Church full of the Holy Ghost Fire will transform anyone that enters the doors or they will flee in resistance. There is no possibility of an experience in which the believer is made a vibrant Christian disciple without the literal ministry of this Divine Person. He is the Fire of God with which the Lord God told John the Baptist that Jesus would baptize His Believers. "He shall baptize you with the Holy Ghost and with fire." (Matthew 3:11c). This generation has witnessed more professing Christians turning away from the Baptism of the Holy Ghost than ever in church history.

"For it is impossible for those who were once enlightened and have tasted of the heavenly gift and were made partakers of the Holy Ghost. And have tasted the good word of God and the powers of the world to come. If they shall fall away, to renew them again unto repentance,

> *seeing they crucify to themselves the Son of God afresh, and put him to an open shame"*

> *Hebrews 6:4-6*

When Apostle Paul warned the church in Hebrews about those that tasted this life-giving ministry but turned away, he declared the danger. He spoke of "seeing they crucify to themselves the Son of God afresh, and put him to an open shame." (Hebrews 6:6b) No one can experience the joy and power of this Baptism in the Holy Ghost and then turn away without consequences.

This is the last of the last days, and every deception in Satan's arsenal is being cast at this generation. Satan hates the Fire of the Holy Ghost because he cannot resist it. Jesus issued us a warning in Matthew.

> *"And because iniquity shall abound, the love of many shall wax cold. But he that shall endure unto the end, the same shall be saved. And this gospel of the kingdom shall be preached in all the world for a witness unto all nations; and then shall the end come."*

> *Matthew 24:12-14*

This word iniquity clearly paints a picture of a church full of compromise and falling away from the deeper life. Iniquity and the fashions of the world are concurrent, and they are robbing the church world of separation to Christ and Godly living. The Fire of the Holy Ghost cannot burn on an altar where the world reigns as king. The Pentecostal Fire that burned for much of the twentieth century was without question manifest in pure and Godly lives. As the churches became bigger and wealthier, they became careless in lifestyle and the world robbed the fire. Starting in the last years of this past century, the Fire of God was replaced with emotional music and cheerleaders in the pulpit. The church world started celebrating the Holy Spirit instead of fasting and praying for His Sovereign visitation. The results have been devastating. Very early in this developing movement, the Catholic Church saw the value of joining forces. Leaders like Katherine Kuhlman welcomed the Catholic priests and nuns in their Catholic attire and with their misguided doctrine to stand equal with them.

Today, the Charismatic world is such a smorgasbord of ideas and experiences that millions of people are left confused and bewildered. The present personalities that represent this part of Pentecost are given to spiritualistic designs and false fire. Ephesus was the first-century church, and Laodicea is the church of today. The first church of Ephesus left their first love within less than one hundred years **(Revelation 2:2-5).** The Laodicea church is described differently, but the problem is the same. They were neither hot nor cold. Both are perfect matches for this present generation of Pentecostals. We are desperate to recover the fire of a mighty Baptism in the Spirit. When the fire is real, many will come to watch us burn and then come under conviction to experience that same joy and knowledge of the Lord. The church of Laodicea certainly represents the multitudes of Pentecostals that no longer even want the Fire of Pentecost. He stated clearly that this crowd is unprepared for His Rapture and will be spewed out into the Tribulation. They are part of the five virgins that had no oil (fire) in their vessels. He called them foolish **(Revelation 3:15-18).**

If you sincerely seek the things of God, you can have them. Those who get in trouble are the hypocrites (false workmen of God), the ones who are dishonest in their hearts toward God. Rather than wanting God to use them, they want to use God's power for their own purposes and to elevate themselves in the eyes of men *(Like the praise of men more than the praise of God John 12:43).* God will not move for people like that, but the devil will. You cannot make a mockery of the things of God and still be His child. However, if you sincerely want the things of God because you love Him, He will answer you at all times. If you are God's property, the devil has no claim on you whatsoever. Use that fiery tongue; hold up the blood-stained banner and tell the story of Jesus without compromise.

The fiery tongue under the power of the Spirit will make men's hearts burn within them. The greatness of His power is being poured out in this final hour. All over the world, people are becoming aware of the need for the baptism of the Holy Ghost. Never has there been an hour such as this! We needn't be concerned about the enemy; nothing can stand against the power of the Holy Ghost in this hour. He wants many witnesses to tell of His greatness. Call on Him in perfect faith, for those who are faithful will see miracle after miracle. The impact of your fiery anointing will do much to win the lost. That fiery anointing will not rest upon you if you are deceived. Keep your eyes on Jesus and His greatness. Don't delight yourself because you are being blessed; delight yourself because you, through that fiery anointing, are blessing others. Joy will come as you delight yourself in your Lord, bowing down to His will the way Jesus did. Let His voice thunder in your ears when you're discouraged. Behold His hand of power that separated the waters of the Red Sea, and know that you have hold of that same hand. He is the God of all flesh, and He walks with you daily; call at any time upon the name of His Son, Jesus, and He will hear. He calls you into His arms to give you His faith, love, strength, and anointing of fire so that He can be poured out to others through you. Receive the baptism of the Holy Ghost and yield to the molding and the shaping of His fire in your life. Amen.

(iv) In a wrong place and with wrong people

All of us in the time past and even recently had looked for God in all the wrong places. It happened when we fell in love with the gifts but forgot the giver (God Himself). Every good gift and every perfect gift is from above and cometh down from the Father of lights, with whom is no variableness, neither shadow of turning (**James 1:17**). Why don't we set our sights just a little bit higher? Wouldn't we want to pursue not just the gifts but also the giver? Many in Christian circles move from crusades to crusades and churches to churches to get healed, get relieved from psychological and spiritual problems, but forget that the greatest miracle is salvation, and it comes from God through His Son, Jesus Christ. Many pastors and prophets are taking the glory of God, but He will not give to another, neither His praise to graven images or man *(Isaiah 42:8).* Many of these false pastors, prophets, and other workmen of God have become personality cults and are marching gullible Christians to hell. Do not worship them or angels but worship God and His Son only.

> ***"And I fell at his feet to worship him. And he said unto me, see thou do it not: I am thy fellow-servant, and of thy brethren that have the testimony of Jesus: worship God: for the testimony of Jesus is the Spirit of prophecy"***
>
> ***Revelation 19:10***

Pastor, prophet, and other workmen of God, you are not the man but Jesus Christ. Jesus is the true bread from Heaven that satisfies our deepest hunger. As I write, many Christians are still following false pastors, prophets, and other workmen of God to hell. Please do not be gullible but become spiritually smart Christians *(Ephesians 5:14)* and know the devices of the enemy *(2 Corinthians 2:11)*. Do not unequally yoke with unbelievers *(2 Corinthians 6:14),* and evil communications corrupt good manners *(1 Corinthians 15:33).*

Awake to righteousness, holiness, and sin not for some have not the knowledge of God: I speak this to your shame *(1 Corinthians 15:34).*

(v) Walking away from spirituality to carnality

We all have the "love at first sight" attitude when we get saved but lose our love for Jesus Christ over time as the going gets tough. Staying with Christ means enjoying good and bad times, mountain-top and valley-bottom lives, and life and death situations. We all make poor calculations on the cost and benefit analyses of following Christ. The spiritual benefits will exceed carnal costs, but in our present dispensation, the opposite is true. The Galatians made miscalculations on the spiritual benefits and carnal costs analysis and found the carnal benefits exceeded the spiritual costs. According to Paul, they made a mistake by walking away from spirituality to carnality.

> ***O foolish Galatians, who hath bewitched you, that ye should not obey the truth, before whose eyes Jesus Christ hath been evidently set forth, crucified among you? Are ye so foolish? Having begun in Spirit, are ye now made perfect by the flesh? Have ye suffered so many things in vain? If it be yet in vain."***

Galatians 3:1, 3-4

It is a wonderful thing to fall in love and get married. But marriage is a relationship, and it takes time and effort to develop and maintain a relationship. It does not matter how deeply you were in love when you married, if you neglect your marriage and devote your attention to other things, your marriage will fail. Marriage is a wonderful gift from God and is worth the time and effort it takes to maintain and deepen that relationship. But salvation is a far greater gift than marriage because it has to do with our eternal destiny. Don't let it drift. Don't neglect it. Don't get distracted with other things, even with good things. Our salvation is so great; we must pay closer attention to it so that we don't drift away from it. It is the one thing that every person needs more than anything else.

In summary, you are either drifting with regard to your salvation because of neglect, or you are growing because of deliberate effort and attention.

What keeps the juice in our salvation from drying is the observation of Romans 12:1-2. The secret of living a holy life boils down to God having control of our minds, bodies, and wills. We can turn around and ask this question. Does God have absolute control of all you have and are? Three possible questions may come out of Roman 12:1-2. First, are you sure you are saved? Second, is your mind being renewed by the transforming power of the Word of God so that the new man on the inside is being permitted to live on the outside? And third, have you discovered and surrendered your life to the will of God?

Paul wants all Christians and the church to develop a heavenly mindset. This will deliver them and the church from much of the earthly preaching filled with deceptive philosophy that was threatening the church at Colosse.

> ***"Beware lest any spoil you through philosophy and vain deceit, after the tradition of men, after the rudiments of the world, and not after Christ"***
>
> ***Colossians 2:8***

Developing a heavenly mindset, as it is written in "the city of God" by St. Augustine, one that thinks of God and his kingdom is very important to us as well.

For as he thinketh in his heart, so is he"

Proverb 23: 9a

Godly thinking leads to having the manifest presence of God in our lives ***(Philippians 4: 8-9)***. Again, godly thinking brings peace and life to us and identifies us as true believers ***(Romans 8:5-6)***. Furthermore, if you are going to live a godly life, it starts with a godly mind ***(Colossians 3: 1-5)***.

This is why Satan is always attacking the believers' minds and thoughts. He wants them to live like the world instead of living like citizens of heaven waiting for their coming King. To develop heavenly mindset and live effective Christian lives, we must focus on our resurrected positions; lead a life of continual discipline, focus on our crucified positions, focus on our hidden life in Christ, and focus on our future in Christ.

5. Get Real with the Word of God

The eternal regret of being almost persuaded will be devastating. Why are many believers becoming almost persuaded and end up losing their salvation? They will miss eternal salvation by a narrow margin because their spirit is willing, but their flesh is weak. There are many like King Agrippa who heard the good news but hardened their hearts until they died prematurely. Therefore, almost persuaded is eternally lost forever. Do not become one of the statistics of almost persuaded believers.

There are four (4) groups of sinners who will miss eternal salvation. They are (a) those who do not need Jesus as Savior because they characterized themselves as good, but no one is good except Jesus *(Ecclesiastes 7:20) and (Romans 3:10)*, (b) those who fear social rejection or harassment —deters people from accepting Christ as Lord and personal Savior. For they love the praise of men more than the praise of God *(John 12:43)*, their status among peers is more important than their relationship with God, (c) Some people like the joy of the present world to eternal things. The parable of the rich young ruler in (Matthew 19: 16-23 perfectly explains this point. He enjoyed his earthly possessions to an eternal relationship with Jesus and (d) many believers resist the Holy Spirit's attempt to convert them to Christ. Stephen told the Pharisees that their behavior was similar to their fathers who resisted the Holy Spirit *(Acts 7:51).* "Ye stiff-necked and uncircumcised in heart and ears, ye do always resist the Holy Ghost, as your fathers did, so do ye"

For true salvation, you must admit that you are a sinner. None is righteous and good. We all deserve to be separated from God and go to hell. God's gift to us is eternal life through Jesus Christ, our Lord. We must believe and receive God's gift of eternal salvation in His terms (not ours) (John 1: 11-13). We must be truly born again in order to go to Heaven. All who go to Heaven must be transformed into the image of Christ before they die.

Repentance is a necessary condition of your salvation *(Acts 3:19).* Repentance turns a person away from sin towards God, and faith turns a person toward God from sin and accepts Jesus Christ as Savior. Repentance and faith are two sides of salvation. Again, repentance results in turning from wickedness and dead works to faith toward God *(Hebrews 6:1).*

To the real Christians, if you choose to put off salvation and die in your sins, you will go to hell remembering that you narrowly refused the opportunity you had today, this week, month, and year to be born again. Salvation is a daily transformation of growing into the very image of Christ. The Lord is actively working in us on holiness and righteousness. Do not resist the work of the Holy Spirit to convert you. If you take your eyes off Jesus, you will sink and lose your salvation. Paul's focus was on Jesus and wanted to know him. To know the Lord, He must first know you. If Jesus Christ does not know you, your salvation is at risk. Spending time daily with the Lord is the key to your salvation. The practice of daily righteousness is proof of your salvation. Also, obedience is an important element of your salvation. Sanctification leads to salvation, but we must be disciplined in order to grow into the image of Christ. Self-righteousness is taking the so-called prophets, pastors, and other workmen of God to hell. Self-righteousness can be a certainty that you are morally superior to others. But God hates self-righteousness because it is a lie. It drives people to pride and separates them from God.

Many Christians have been in churches forever and still do not have a relationship with God. They profess they know Him, but God does not know them. Moreover, profession alone is not enough for your salvation. You must be a true born-again Christian. This is well captured in Titus 1:16, "They profess that they know God; but in works they deny him, being abominable and disobedient, and into every good work reprobate. Watch ye therefore, and pray always, that ye may be accounted, worthy to escape all these things that shall come to pass and to stand before the Son of man (Luke 21:36).

Often in our lives, we find ourselves in situations where we do not know what to do. The circumstances of life have swirled out of control, and the pressure is overwhelming. But the promise of God is that at that moment, He does what needs to be done. He will not leave us alone; He will not forget we need Him. The Father stands with us, and we never face the music alone. That security brings us hope. That hope is a precious gift given to us because Jesus lives.

My plea and cry for all sinners, especially my Christian friends and myself included, as apostle Paul made a plea for his Jewish brothers and sisters in the book of Romans [Romans 1:16; Romans 9: 1-24; Romans 10: 1-3; and Roman 11: 26-30] is that they being ignorant of God's righteousness and going about to establish their own righteousness, and have not submitted themselves unto the righteousness of God might be saved.

And if you are not aflame with the baptism of fire, you, too, are failing Him again and again. The baptism of fire must burn within you. The anointing of the Holy Spirit will make Christ come alive in your innermost being so that you will not be an imitation of Him. You will have HIM on the inside— no longer will you be striving to work for Him in your own strength. Jesus, through the power of the Holy Ghost, will be working through you. Perhaps it is not within your own ability to be a witness for the Lord, but the Holy Ghost is able to be that witness when He lives in you and you let Him work through you. The Holy Ghost can witness, preach, pray—all you need do is yield yourself to Him.

6. Final Thoughts

God is warning all believing Christians that no one knows when their appointed time to die would be. He is pleading with all of us to trust Christ while we are still alive. At-risk Christians, don't you know that you are going down to hell and bear the dreadful wrath of God that is now angry with you every day and every night. Therefore, let everyone that is out of Christ now awake and fly from the wrath to come. If you do not know Christ today, hell is your final destination. Flee from that future and take refuge by faith in Jesus. Often in our lives, we find ourselves in situations where we do not know what to do. The circumstances of today's life have swirled out of control, and the pressure is overwhelming. But the promise of God is that at the moment, He does what needs to be done. Our loving Father will not leave us alone; He will not forget we need Him. The Father stands with us, and we never face the music alone. That security brings us hope. That hope is a precious gift given to us because Jesus lives.

The second part of salvation is predestination. God knew the elect before they were born. God chose those He knew in a saving relationship and conformed them to the image of

Christ. Good examples of the elect are Isaiah *(Isaiah 6:8)*, Jeremiah *(Jeremiah 1:5),* Samuel, Paul, and many more. God called them as they heard the gospel, and they responded in faith. He then justified them- declaring them righteous, and glorified them as saved forever *(Romans 8:29-30).*

The end product of Christianity is the attainment of the image of Christ. Without salvation, your Christian life is worthless. Salvation is a free gift of God, but it will cost you everything. God gives us faith to work on our holiness and righteousness, but He is working on us all the time to attain Jesus' image. The power to work on your own salvation comes from our loving God, who leads, and we follow. Our everyday focus is heavenward, as St. Augustine envisioned in his book entitled "The city of God"

The most sobering verses in the New Testament are *(Matthew 7:21-23).* These verses are not written for the unsaved world but for the Christians, including the workmen of God (pastors, prophets, Elders, and more) who are self-righteous and have false knowledge of eternal salvation.

My plea and cry for all sinners, especially my folks in Africa, Ghana and myself included, as apostle Paul made a plea for his Jewish brothers and sisters in the book of Romans [Romans 1:16; Romans 9: 1-24; Romans 10: 1-3; and Roman 11: 26-30] is that they being ignorant of God's righteousness and going about to establish their own righteousness, and have not submitted themselves unto the righteousness of God might be saved.

As a Christian, I am not a "sinner saved by grace". I was a sinner saved by grace at the point of salvation. Once I was saved and transformed. I am now a new creature in Christ, fully capable of living faithfully and fruitfully for Him.

7. Let's Pray

Dear God, I [*insert your name about here*] come to you to receive your son Jesus Christ as my Lord and personal Savior. I thank you for sending Jesus Christ to die for my sins. I [*insert your name about here*] acknowledge that I do not deserve your favor. Father, I thank you that the Lord Jesus Christ died and paid for all my sins on the cross. Lord, even my salvation is a free gift without works; it cost the whole of your life. It is free for me now, but it will cost me all my life to preserve till I see you in heaven. Father, I thank you that Jesus' ultimate sacrifice on the cross paid the full penalty of all my sins and guilt. Thank you again for accepting His sacrifice and raising him from the dead. Father God, I [*insert your name about here*] ask you now to forgive all of my sins and give me eternal life. Come into my life, I pray and live in my life. Give me faith to believe and to trust in your Son Jesus Christ, forever, so that I may live for you here and that I [*insert your name about here*] may go to be with you for all of eternity. Father God, crucify anything in me that would remove my name from the book of life in the name of Jesus.

Through the blood of Jesus, I am justified, sanctified, and made holy with God's holiness and righteousness. Lord, help us to grasp and know your great love. O God of victory, grant me the lost grace for repentance. Righteous Savior, thank you for your unconditional love. It is because of this great love that I live in the freedom that Jesus has given me. Use me, [***insert your name about here***] as your vessel to go and preach an unadulterated salvation message to my family members, friends, and the rest of the world. Sovereign Lord, I pray that you send your Holy Spirit to convict and convert the hearts of all those I preach face-to-face and online.

Heavenly Father, I pray that my behavior and my lifestyle reflect you. I [***insert your name about here]*** remain a righteous being, doing things that are acceptable in your sight. I pray that when I fall short, I do not remain in a place of carnality. I declare that I will pursue the paths of righteousness. I pray that I continue to delight in your law, meditating on it day and night. Lord, I want to be like the tree planted along the riverbank, bearing good fruit. I, [***insert your name about here]*** pray that I will never wither and that I prosper in all that I do. Righteous God, I seek you with all my heart; do not let me stray from your commandments neither through ignorance nor by willful disobedience. I have treasured and stored your word in my heart so that I will not sin against you. I pray that you strengthen me so that I can become spiritually mature and more like you in every aspect of my life. I declare that I will remain on your path of righteousness.

Open my spiritual eyes to see that heaven is my ultimate home and the world is my temporary home. Grant me [***insert your name about here]*** inner spiritual strength to resist temptations and to control my mind. Your Word never dies, and it remains the same till now *(Hebrews 13:8).* May God grant me wisdom and make me strong. Let me, *[insert your name about here]* abide in you forever and ever.

Jesus Christ defeated the whole kingdom of darkness and won an overwhelming victory by disarming principalities and powers at the cross. Jesus Christ is the victor. He is the mighty conqueror. Jesus triumphed over all his foes, and he has given me complete victory over every foe in my life. This includes a victory over Satan, the demons, and the whole kingdom of darkness, as well as victory over all works of darkness, including witches and wizards. Therefore, Satan, demons, witches, and warlocks, you have absolutely no power and no authority over me *(Luke 10:19).* Lord of glory; let your kingdom come through the power of the Holy Spirit and the glory of God. I *[insert your name about here]* seal this prayer with the precious blood of the Great Shepherd of the sheep and thanksgiving. In Jesus' name, I pray, Amen.

Chapter 2
The Lost in the Lost Church

"Not every One that saith unto me, Lord, Lord, shall enter into the kingdom of heaven, but he that doeth the will of my Father which is in heaven. Many will say to me in that day, Lord, Lord, have we not prophesied in thy name, and in thy name have cast out devils? And in thy name doing many wonderful works? And then will I profess unto them, I never knew you: depart from me, ye that work iniquity"

-Mathew 7:21-23.

"Then Jesus said unto them, take heed and beware of the leaven of the Pharisees and of the Sadducees"

Matthew 16:6

"I know thy works, that thou art neither cold nor hot: I would thou wert cold or hot. So then because thou art lukewarm, and neither cold nor hot, I will spue thee out of my mouth. Because thou sayest, I am rich, and increased

with goods, and have need of nothing, and knowest not that thou art wretched, and miserable, and poor, and blind, and naked"

Revelation 3:15

"For the pastors are become brutish, and have not sought the lord: therefore, they shall not prosper, and all their flocks shall be scattered"

Jeremiah 10:21

Wherefore seeing we also are compassed about with so great a cloud of witnesses, let us lay aside every weight, and the sin which doth so easily beset us, and let us run with patience the race that set before us. Looking unto Jesus the author and finisher of our faith; who for the joy that was set before him endured the cross, despising the shame, and is set down at the right had of throne of God"

Hebrews 12:12

1. Introduction:

I am writing this chapter in tears and fear because nearly 98 percent of churchgoers (including myself) are lost in the lost church. The church is not preaching and teaching the wholesome word of God anymore. There is misinformation and disinformation of the gospel on the part of the pastors, preachers, and prophets who are throwing dust in the eyes of believers. Many churches and pastors minimize the message of the lord in an effort to make the congregation comfortable in their sins. Many pastors in the pulpits are not called by God but invite themselves to the ministry of God for either popularity or other monetary gains. The church has lost its neutrality in the pursuit of the truth. On one hand, it has been swayed to the extreme right by following the Far-right and neo-Nazi ideologies. On the other hand, it is tilted too much to the left by aligning itself to extreme liberal policies, such as Lesbian, Gay, Bisexual, and Transgender (LGBT) ideologies. Madness is taking over clarity and sanity in the church. The church is facing much more moral crisis than ever. Truth is taken as lies, while lies have become the truth. Lies become the truth if the church and Christians allow them. There is more opposition to telling the truth than lies. Chaos is gradually increasing in our churches, and God's judgment is eminent.

Today, the presence of God is missing in our churches because of the lack of unity of purpose in our gatherings. For convenience's sake, many workmen of God are flipping to the enemy's side by preaching and teaching the works of flesh listed in ***Galatians 5:19-21.*** Things are continually falling apart in the church as I go to the press.

God has given every man his free will, and it is unfortunate that many live in uncleanness, in the lust of their hearts to dishonor their bodies among themselves (Tattoos). Tattoos have become more popular than ever because Satan and his demons know that the Lord's Second Coming is drawing near. These demons are enticing and seducing men and women (rich, or poor, black or white, small or big,) especially Christians from apostate-thinking states to tattooing. Once they get the bodies of Christians with indelible marks, their spirits will naturally succumb to their tricks and traps. We have to exhibit godly courage to stand strong in the faith. We cannot overcome Satan's seducing spirit that grips the world if we are cowards. We are soldiers in God's army and cannot stand down on biblical issues out of fear of being labeled a homophobe or judge. Sin is at the very heart of all that is against Almighty God. Jealousy is the very sin that caused Lucifer to rebel against God. Many Christians are hypocrites because many are both public-worshippers and secret-sinners *(Matthew 15:8).* The lost Church must remove their self-interest (secret sins) and seek out the will of God.

What kind of worship are we offering God? How can part-time Christians fight a full-time devil? Churchgoers are not true Christians. They look for miracles from church to church. Also, they stay offended, unforgiving, spiritually blinded, spiritually proud and weak. Things are also falling apart for Christians who walk away from sound biblical doctrine. There is, therefore, a greater need to pray for the lost and backsliders across racial, national, and cultural boundaries because the kingdom of God is inclusive.

2. The lost in the Church

Even many religious people who believe in Jesus Christ will find themselves lost.

"Not everyone that saith unto me, Lord, Lord, shall enter into the kingdom of heaven: but he that doeth the will of my Father which is in heaven. Many will say to me in that day, Lord, Lord, have we not prophesied in thy name? And in thy name have cast out devils? And in thy name done many wonderful works? And then will I profess unto them, I never knew you: depart from me, ye that work iniquity"

Matthew7:21-23

Peter is also warning us about the fiery judgment of the ungodly if we do not repent and make a quick turn to the Lord Jesus Christ *(2 Peter 3:7-12).*

The Second coming of the Lord can happen at any moment from now, so put your houses in order. We claim salvation only in Jesus Christ. Nearly 98 percent of the churchgoers and workmen of God are neither cold nor hot. They are Christians for a moment, and the next moment, they are not. They are compromisers of the bible by turning left and right. They are more of the World than of the Lord. Paul was warning us in his first letter to Timothy that:

"Now the Spirit speaketh expressly, that in the latter times some shall depart from the faith, giving heed to seducing spirits, and doctrines of devils. Speaking lies in hypocrisy; having their conscience seared with a hot iron"

1 Timothy 4:1-2

Those who depart from the faith are the lost in the lost church. They are the tares among the wheat, which will be cast into the fiery furnace by the angels.

The wicked, including the lost in the church, will be alive in the fire, weeping and gnashing their teeth in eternity. They will be faced with the saddest biblical text.

> ***"And whosoever was not found written in the book of life was cast into the lake of fire"***
>
> ***Revelation 20:15***

Judgment is awaiting us and many of us who feel saved. We are going to have a rude awakening when the Lord's trumpet sounds. There will be weeping and gnashing of teeth because many of us who feel heaven-bound would be surprised to find ourselves with the wicked in hell. Most of the weeping and gnashing of teeth would come from the so-called Christians who might think they made it to heaven. They are fooling themselves on earth because they have created their own righteousness and holiness outside the Lord's. They are still chilling out with false prophets and teachers who prophesied and taught them lies. True believers of Christ worship Him in truth and spirit *(John 4:24)*.

Everywhere you go these days, you meet people who call themselves Christians (Christ-like people). Are they true Christians or just using the wrong-name tags? The first-century Christians were 'set apart for Christ. They talked, walked, and carried their crosses daily like Christ. These Christians carried spiritual mindsets. They were transformed into new creatures, studied, spoke, and taught the word of God (prophetic public proclamation), and had a constant visitation of the Lord. These Christians had power and authority, and their proclamations were effective. Whatever Paul, Peter, John, and the rest said came to pass.

> *"Insomuch that they brought forth the sick into the streets, and laid them on beds and couches, that at the least the shadow of Peter passing by might overshadow some of them. There came also a multitude out of the cities round about unto Jerusalem, bringing sick folks, and them which were vexed with unclean spirits and they were healed everyone."*

> *Acts 5:15-16*

Why are today's Christians powerless? We have become either part-time Christians or Sunday- Christians. We have been conformed to the world, so we put away the word of God in public places. We cannot mix the word of God and the world system because they are different from each other.

> *"Making the word of God of none effect through your tradition, which ye have delivered and many such like things do ye"*

> *Mark 7:13*

In Paul's defense in the book of Acts, King Agrippa did not want to become a Christian because it would have meant a 'set apart' life for Christ. This worldly king knew the high qualities of a true Christian and was not prepared to give up all his worldly treasures. Most Christians are serving two masters (Christ and the world). They go to church and still gossip, fornicate, steal, commit adultery and engage in all kinds of the works of the flesh. Matthew has warned us about the delicate balancing of Christ and the world.

> ***"No man can serve two masters, for either he will hate the one, and love the other, or else he will hold to the one, and despise the other. Ye cannot serve God and Mammon"***
>
> ***Matthew 6:24***

I have always believed in the philosophy that whatever you do in life, do it with all your heart, mind, and soul. You cannot give 99 percent to Christ and one percent to the world. Christianity is 100 percent business, so if you are not ready now, do not come to Christ. A faulty balance is an abomination to God (Proverbs 11:1).It is a sheer waste of time to pretend to be a Christian because the sin of presumption is a great abomination to God. Christianity is measured at both heart and outward. Faith without works is dead. Faith must correlate with works and vice versa. Phony Christians tend to show their works in the Lord by praising and glorifying God. Those who scream at the top of their voices could be possible candidates for phony Christians.

Phony Christians may not deny Christ in public places, but in works, they deny Him. They profess they know God, but they also engage in the works of the flesh. You cannot tell the difference in lifestyles between a phony Christian and an unbeliever. When the woman with the spirit of divination in the book of Acts saw Paul and Silas, she knew that they were the servants of the Most High God who showed people the way of salvation. Can a stranger identify you as a Christian without you telling him about your faith? If the answer is no, then you may be a candidate for phony Christian. There is an aroma of Christ or anointing on every true Christian because of the presence of the Holy Spirit in us.

> ***"For we are unto God a sweet savor of Christ, in them that are saved and in them that perish".***

> ***2 Corinthians 2:15***

There are millions of born-again Christians by profession, but in the works, they deny Christ and the word of God. These phony Christians are bible-sized devils because, in works, they promote Satan and demons. Many phony Christians who hide in their faith are afraid of men more than God.

> ***"For they loved the praise of men more than the praise of God"***

> ***John 12:43***

Most phony Christians get angry and bitter if you try to instruct, teach and direct them to true Christianity. They will quickly quote you as follows;

"Judge not that ye not be judged"

Matthew 7:1

They are making errors because they are not balancing the whole scriptures. Christians are expected to judge their brethren but not the world because Christ will judge the world.

"For what have I to judge them also that is without? Do not ye judge them that are within? But them that are without God judgeth. Therefore, put away from among yourselves that wicked person"

1 Corinthians 5:12-13

There is a long tail of misconception and misunderstanding on the judgment of one servant by another. When a Christian corrects, instructs, teaches, and directs a brother to holiness of God, pastors, elders, and fellow Christians tend to disagree. They call this Christian divisive, but they are wrong if they do not balance the whole scriptures. Judgment must first begin in the House of God (1 Peter 4:17). For anyone to say that I am not going to judge what you say and do is totally irresponsible. Satan is using the same scriptures through phony Christians to accuse true Christians who teach the true word of God. Satan is the accuser of the brethren and never stops accusing us before our Father in heaven. Paul warns us about such an accusation.

> **"If any man teaches otherwise, and consent not to wholesome words, even the words of our Lord Jesus Christ, and to the doctrine which is according godliness, he is proud, knowing nothing, but doting about questions and strife of words, whereof cometh envy, strife, railings, evil surmising"**
>
> **1 Timothy 6:3-4**

Note that, we are commanded to know, discern, determine, prove and test all spirits (1 John 1:4). Jesus was not kidding when He said with tears that after His departure men in sheep skin would creep into the church to deceive the sheep. Satan has his people inside the church of Jesus Christ now, transforming themselves into angels of light with the ultimate aim of carrying millions to hell. Paul warned us that they are deceiving and being deceived themselves. We have a duty as true Christians to identify these phonies among us and help them receive quality salvation. Ignorance creates bondage and illiterate Christians. Ignorance is a sin and many so-called Christians will end up in hell because of the former. Ignorance is not an excuse for breaking the laws of God. Let us become like the Christians in Philippi and Thessalonica, who searched the scriptures every day. 2 Corinthians 2:15:

> **"These were more noble than those in Thessalonica, in that they received the word with all readiness of mind, and searched the scriptures daily, whether those things were so"**
>
> **Acts 17:11**

Many so-called Christians have created their own gods and offer prayers to these gods. Many are frustrated because these self-made gods do not answer their prayers. They trust men more than the Creator God. They are fooled into believing that they are heaven-bound.

> ***"A wonderful and horrible thing is committed in the land; the prophets prophesy falsely, and the priests bear rule by their means; and my people love to have it so, and what will ye do in the end thereof?***
>
> ***Jeremiah 5:30-31.***

> ***"For the time will come when they will not endure sound doctrine; but after their own lusts shall they heap to themselves teachers; having itching ears, and they shall turn away their ears from the truth, shall turn unto fables"***
>
> ***2 Timothy 4:3-4***

The lost in the church are not different from the lost church because they harken to false prophets, diviners, dreamers, enchanters, and sorcerers. They are practicing religion (not Christianity) which is the highest form of hypocrisy. Religion has become a manipulating tool to deceive, control, and suppress most Christians. It was used in the slave trade in Africa and Americas, and is being used today in many parts of the world, particularly in Africa, to exploit the lost Christians. Pastors and prophets are profiting from the church by selling to the congregation water, oil, and many products made in the name of Jesus.

3. The Lost Church

Many churches and denominations are out of steps with sound doctrine by indulging in false teaching, adulterated worship, and patronizing in wrong teaching to satisfy their egos as well as whims and caprices. These large crops of preachers and prophets are cashing in on their congregations. It is all about church business and not soul winning. Many also engage in merchandising their products to the sick and the lost in the form of the blood of Jesus. The blood of Jesus is too precious to sell to anyone.

> ***"Heal the sick, cleanse the lepers, raise the dead, cast out devils; freely ye have received, freely give"***
>
> *Matthew 10:8*

The lost church is made up of pastors, prophets, evangelists, ministers, the clergy, and including the congregation who have lost their first love and have gone after strange spirits. Most of them have lied, manipulated, and deceived their congregations and each other. They argue that righteousness is relative and within the individual. If the church doctrine has question marks, get out fast. We must be vigilant to the doctrine that is being taught. It must align with the will and the laws of God. The Scriptures must balance. All truth is parallel. God of the Supernatural is also God of the natural. You cannot pick one truth and run away with it.

Many workmen of God are not teaching and preaching the true doctrine of God almighty. They cut the truth into pieces (concision of words) and lead many astray. They are blind themselves and continue to lead many blind Christians to hell. If the doctrine of the ministers of the Gospel is different from sound one, they must be removed from the church and never taught. The false workmen of God conceal their true motives. Their true characters may hide in deep dark secrets. Past examples of such characters in the United States of America are Jim Jones, David Koresh, the Bakers, and many more modern-day Televangelists. We must question their motives to avoid Church disasters. Many of their motives can be discerned, but many more are hidden in the use of the Gospel. For instance, if they preach about going to selling in the church of the Lord and Jesus was driving money changers in the Church then something is obviously wrong with these workmen of God.

> ***And said unto them, it is written, my house shall be called the house of Prayer; but ye have made it a den of thieves"***
>
> ***Matthew 21:13***

Today, "patience and longsuffering" have been removed from the pulpits and replaced with "miracles and prosperity". The lost Church is turning its back on sound doctrine and turning toward the sinful world in order not to offend nor cause an uproar among the people. Many churches are afraid of agents of Satan that try to infiltrate the body of the Church. A good example of modern-day agitators in the church of the Lord is equal rights for homosexuals. What a man does outside the Church is one thing, but to claim that his lifestyle has a right to be recognized as righteous within the Church is another. Sinners and the lost are welcome to the Church, but their membership in the Church, their salvation and calling, must align with the laws of God and not the opinions of the American Civil Liberties and Union (ACLU), nor the laws of man. We are to be held and steadfast in our profession of faith.

> ***Till we all come in the unity of the faith, and of the knowledge of the Son of God, unto a perfect man, unto the measure of the stature of the fullness of Christ. That we henceforth be no more children, tossed to and fro, and carried about with every wind of doctrine, by the sleight of men and cunning craftiness, whereby they lie in wait to deceive"***

> ***Ephesians 4:13-14***

The lost church must remove their self-interest, no more being afraid of telling the truth and seeking out the will of God concerning the church. Thus, rich churches must remove the silos and come together with the poor ones in faith, hope, and love. The lost church must come to the spiritual realization that everything we see is temporal and not eternal, and all will burn away and decay. Let the church and the lost in the church dream and think of the city of God every day.

Today's churches are after large and beautiful buildings with a large membership, but Jesus was not after big crowds but devoted converts who were willing to follow him even unto death. Eleven of the twelve disciples of Jesus were killed and martyred for the cause of preaching and spreading the gospel of good news for all men (a command Christ gave to His church). The lost church is declining fast because it has huge crowds who are only happy with messages that they want to hear. We need ministers of the gospel who preach the word of God with Holy fire and Holy conviction. While some preachers make ear-tickling sermons that last a few days, others speak the words of God that last generations to come. Some of the preachers whose messages have lasted for years include Charles H. Spurgeon, C.S Lewis, only to mention but few.

The church is falling apart all over the world including Africa, Europe, and the United States of America because it lacks fire, power, holiness, and hearing from God. The church has eloquent preachers, state of the art technology in preaching, but it still lacks godliness and power. The church should submit to Jesus and seek His approval instead of man. The church is sleeping and in the doldrums because Great Revivals are not bringing in holy convictions. As the church continues to witness trials, tribulations, and hard times, only those who are marked and moved by the power and glory of God will be the ones who will stand and speak with thunder and with great power. The holiness and righteousness of Jesus are taken as a joke and mocks God. Holiness and righteousness to the lost and lost church is a thing of the past (Old Testament mentality). Jesus gave us power over all the power of the enemy, after His resurrection, but we cannot use it because of lack or non-existence of holiness and righteousness.

> ***"Behold, I give unto you power to tread on serpents and scorpions, and overall the power of the enemy; and nothing shall by any means hurt you"***
>
> ***Luke 10:19***

If you have no good standing in the Lord, the enemy has power over you. We see Satan running many churches and chasing after the children of God in the Lord's own churches. Why? The devil knows true Christians and fake ones. If you are not a real Christian, don't mess with Satan *(Acts 19:15-17).* It is about time the congregation and the churches exercise their God-given power over the enemy to magnify the name of the Lord. The church of the Lord is falling apart because of the false understanding of Holiness and false understanding of the great power of the Holy Spirit.

Many churches are only subject to the voices of the prophets and other workmen of God. Consequently, they cannot hear from God. They are using their personal agendas to please people instead of God. Churches all over the world have become entertainment centers and dancing halls to please themselves. When the church opens its ears to the Holy Spirit and the will of God, then we will witness the revival and transformation of the Church of Jesus Christ.

4. Satan goes to church

Meanwhile, agents of Satan are found in every living church. Their job is simply to hinder the spread of the gospel in order to weaken the Church of the Lord. There are people who have been under the bondage of Satan, people who have allowed the enemy of their souls to come and take control of their lives and pull them away from their allegiance to Christ. You have been around the gospel all of your life, your friends have told you about Jesus, your wife has told you about Jesus, your husband has told you about Jesus, and you just keep resisting. Do you know why you resist? Because Satan doesn't want to lose you to God's kingdom. And he will fight everything he can to keep you from accepting Jesus Christ because when you accept Jesus Christ, he knows that is when life really begins for you. In today's culture, there is an incredible rise of Satanism and demonism all throughout the world. As we look at what is happening in our culture today, we should not be surprised to observe the increase of all of these things that are involved in spiritual warfare because 1 Timothy tells us that "the Spirit expressly says that in later times some will depart from the faith," now watch this, "giving heed to deceiving spirits and to doctrines of demons". In the 9th chapter of the book of Revelation, John the revelatory tells us that during the Tribulation, there is going to be an outpouring of the demonology of demons in the Tribulation period. I don't know if you've ever read the description of what happens, but when you get a chance sometime, read Revelation 9:8 through 11, and there, you will find a description of what happens when the demons of hell are let loose on the planet Earth during the Tribulation period.

Did you know that Satan's purpose is to divide and conquer? Satan has always been a divider. When he was cast out of heaven, he divided the angels, and he took a third of them with him. He instigated division in the first family, pitting Cain against Abel. In the early church, he entered into the heart of Ananias and motivated him to divide his loyalty between God and money. Wherever you see Satan at work, there is always division. Listen to me carefully. Did you ever wonder why there are so many churches that go through church splits and have all kinds of problems? It is because Satan is at work in the midst of the church. You say, "You mean, Satan goes to church"? Oh my, yes. He goes to church. I have probably sat next to him a couple of times. And he loves to divide the people of God. If we could only understand that, we would step back from our petty differences and realize that we're just playing into the hand of our enemy, whose purpose is to divide. What happens in churches is that Satan gets a hold of the tongues of God's people, and he uses their tongues to poison the atmosphere of the church. And he does that in families, and he does it in workplaces, and he does it in communities. Satan's purpose is to divide. He does not know the meaning of unity. He has no concept of unity. His whole strategy is the strategy of division. He is the great deceiver, and he is the great divider.

5. Get Real with the Word

The church pursues holiness, starting with Spirit-empowered, self-discipline, where people grow to be more like Jesus. The heart of self-discipline is discipleship. Leaders use Scripture to teach, correct, train, and equip Christians to be holy people who continually grow in Christlikeness. When believers sin, they are supposed to confess and repent, and others are to lovingly and humbly walk with them to help them grow in grace. Billions await Jesus Christ's Return to set up the Kingdom of God. But few know how He will do this. It will not happen the way most expect. A big surprise awaits many of us who call ourselves Christians. Madness is taking over clarity and sanity in the church. The church is facing much more moral crisis than ever. Truth is taken as lies, while lies have become the truth. Lies become the truth if the church and Christians allow them. There is more opposition to telling the truth than lies. Chaos is gradually increasing in our churches, and God's judgment is eminent.

The reason nobody holds the church in high regard anymore is that its members look no different from those in the world they are trying to convert. The church of Jesus Christ has lost its passion for preaching the gospel. We will not see the true power of God until we embrace the lost personal holiness, righteousness of God, and hearing from God.

The lost and the church are one in one because members make up the church. If the lost is rotten, the church is rotten. As the enemy attacks, the church membership goes down, so goes down the church. Remember Satan beguiles, seduces, opposes, resists, deceives, causes confusion, hinders, buffets, tempts, persecutes, blasphemes, fights, and manipulates with an end game of destroying the Church of Jesus Christ.

Satanists in the churches use women to go after men of God and destroy them through sex and money. Once you smite the shepherd (the pastors or prophets), the congregation will easily be scattered.

> **"Awake, O sword, against my shepherd, and against the man that is my fellow, saith the Lord of hosts: smite the shepherd, and the sheep shall be scattered: and I will turn mine hand upon the little ones"**
>
> **Zechariah 13:7**

The prophetesses with Jezebel spirit are teaching and seducing God's servants to commit fornication and eat things sacrificed unto idols.

> **"Notwithstanding I have a few things against thee because thou sufferest that woman Jezebel which called herself prophetess, to teach and seduce my servants to commit fornication, and to eat things sacrificed unto idols"**
>
> **Revelation2:20.**

Many ministries of God are losing their anointing and flames of fire because of sex and fornication. Lucifer is attacking the choir and music ministries by making their members commit fornication and adultery.

God has given every man his free will, and it is unfortunate that many live in uncleanness, in the lust of their hearts to dishonor their bodies among themselves (Tattoos). Tattoos have become more popular than ever because Satan and his demons know that the Lord's Second Coming is drawing near. These demons are enticing and seducing men and women (rich or poor, black or white, small or big), especially Christians from apostate-thinking states to tattooing. Once they get the bodies of Christians, their spirits will naturally succumb to their tricks and traps.

There are millions of born-again Christians by profession, but in the works, they deny Christ and the word of God. These phony Christians are bible-sized devils because, in works, they promote Satan and demons. Many phony Christians who hide in their faith are afraid of men more than God.

Many so-called Christians have created their own gods and offer prayers to these gods. Many are frustrated because these self-made gods do not answer their prayers. They trust men more than the Creator God. They are fooled into believing that they are heaven-bound.

The lost church is made up of pastors, prophets, evangelists, ministers, the clergy, and including the congregation who have lost their first love and have gone after strange spirits. Most of them have lied, manipulated, and deceived their congregations and each other. They argue that righteousness is relative and within the individual. If the church has misguided doctrine get out fast. We must be vigilant to the doctrine that is being taught. It must align with the will and the laws of God. The Scriptures must balance. All truth is parallel. God of the Supernatural is also God of the natural. You cannot pick one truth and run away with it.

The church is sleeping and in the doldrums because Great Revivals are not bringing in holy convictions. As the church continues to witness trials, tribulations, and hard times, only those who are marked and moved by the power and glory of God will be the ones who will stand and speak with thunder and with great power. The holiness and righteousness of Jesus are taken as a joke and mocks God. Holiness and righteousness to the lost and lost church is a thing of the past (Old Testament mentality). Jesus gave us power over all the power of the enemy after His resurrection, but we cannot use it because lack or non-existence of holiness and righteousness.

6. Final Thoughts

Today, Jesus is renowned all over the world, commonly known in one way or another in every culture of the world, whether one professes to be Christian, atheist, or of any other religion. Many have positive comments about Him, regardless of their beliefs about who He was and what He taught. His name also stirs controversy and debate. Yet, despite worldwide recognition—despite billions professing to be His followers—despite all the knowledge circulating about Him—Jesus Christ remains unknown—even to Christianity. These are those that are lost within themselves, believing that they are righteous and just in their eyes but cannot justify themselves before God.

The church is falling apart all over the world including Africa, Europe, and the United States of America because it lacks fire, power, holiness, and hearing from God. The church should submit to Jesus and seek His approval instead of man.

Satanic ministers can be found in every living church. Their job is to hinder, and if possible, destroy the work of God. Many of their women go after the men of God, seeking to destroy them through sex and money because they know that when you smite, they shepherd and the sheep shall be scattered *(Zechariah 13:7).*

God desires perfection in all our endeavors, including serving and worshiping Him.

> *"And when Abram was ninety years old and nine, the Lord appeared to Abram and said unto him, I am Almighty God; walk before me, and be thou perfect"*
>
> *Genesis 17:1*

> *"Be ye therefore perfect, even as your Father, which is in heaven is perfect"*
>
> *Matthew 5:48*

God demands a perfect church before the Lord's Second Coming. It is true, the church is falling apart and confused, but God will align the church's goals with His will. Furthermore, the church desires the completeness of God's word and excellence in righteousness by releasing joy, love, peace, grace, and kindness. In the end times, churches will become imitators and followers of God. Finally, the church will come to a mature state and bear fruits. When the Lord Jesus Christ and the Holy Spirit are drivers of our church, we are riding in a perfect ship.

7. Let's Pray.

Thank you for assuring me *[Insert your name about here]* that you will build your church and the gates of hell cannot prevail against it *(Matthew 16:18)*. O Lord, transfer, remove or change human agents who vowed to stop the advancement of your church. In the name of the Father of our Lord Jesus Christ, Satan you cannot beguile, seduce, oppose, resist, deceive, cause confusion, hinder, buffet, tempt, persecute, fight, and manipulate us with the end game of destroying the Church of Jesus Christ.

I *[Insert your name about here]* nullify every effect of the bite of sexual perversion upon this church in the name of Jesus. Let our eyes be delivered from lust in the name of Jesus. I *[insert your name about here]* bind and put to flight, the spirit of fear, anxiety, and discouragement, in the name of Jesus Christ. I take the shield of faith to quench every fiery dart of the enemy in the name of Jesus. I *[insert your name about here]* pray for mighty revival and the zeal for the gospel to be preached in all the corners of the earth because many believers are discouraged. This is not the time to stop praying and fasting. Father, help me seek you more than ever because the Queen of harlot has entered the church to snack, steal, and destroy the shepherds and the sheep.

Let the eyes of our understanding be enlightened, that we might know the hope of our calling, the riches of the glory of our inheritance in the saints, and exceeding greatness of your power toward us, who believe *(Ephesians 1:17-18).* Strengthen us with might by your Spirit in the inner man *(Ephesians 3:16).* Father God, I *[insert your name about here]* know that I have broken your laws, and my sins have separated me from you. I am very sorry, and now I want to turn away from my past sinful life toward you. Please forgive me, and help me avoid sinning again. I believe that your son, Jesus Christ died, for my sins, was resurrected from the dead, is alive, and hears my prayer.

I *[insert your name about here]* invite Jesus to become the Lord of my life, to rule and reign in my heart from this day forward. Please send your Holy Spirit to help me obey You and to do Your will for the rest of my life. In Jesus' name, I pray, Amen.

Every evil door that is giving my enemies way in my life be closed now by the blood of Jesus in the name of Jesus. I *[insert your name about here]* use the blood of Jesus to lose myself from every spirit in me which is not a Spirit of God in the name of Jesus. Let the divine anointing for spiritual breakthrough fall upon me now, in the name of Jesus. I shall not die, but live, and declare the works of the Lord *(Psalm 118:17).* I *[insert your name about here]* receive power to operate with sharp spiritual eyes that cannot be deceived in the name of Jesus. Let the glory and power of the Almighty God fall upon my life in a mighty way, in the name of Jesus.

Jesus Christ defeated the whole kingdom of darkness and won an overwhelming victory by disarming principalities and powers at the cross. Jesus is the victor. He is a mighty conqueror. Jesus triumphed over all his foes, and he has given me complete victory over every foe in my life. This includes a victory over Satan, demons, and the whole kingdom of darkness, as well as victory over all works of darkness, including witches and wizards. Therefore, Satan, demons, witches, and warlocks, you have absolutely no power and no authority over me. Lord Jesus, let your kingdom come in the power of the Holy Spirit and glory of God. I *[insert your name about here]* seal this prayer with the precious blood of the Great Shepherd of the sheep and with thanksgiving. Amen.

Chapter 3
Do not compromise your faith & Salvation

"Only be thou strong and very courageous, that thou mayest observe to do according to all the law, which Moses my servant commanded thee: turn not from it to the right hand or to the left, that thou mayest prosper whithersoever thou goest"

Joshua 1:7

"Every word of God is pure; he is a shield unto them that put their trust in him. Add thou not unto his words, lest he reprove thee, and thou be found a liar"

Proverbs 30:5-6

"Salvation belongeth unto the Lord: thy blessing is upon thy people"

Psalm 3:8

"For I testify unto every man that heareth the words of the prophecy of this book, if any man shall add unto these things, God shall add unto

him the plagues that are written in this book. And if any man shall take away from the words of the book of this prophecy, God shall take away his part out of the book of life, and out of the holy city, and from the things which are written in this book"

Jeremiah 33:1

"Woe unto you, when all men shall speak well of you! For so did their fathers to the false prophets"

Luke 6:26

"But let your communication be, Yea, yea, and Nay, nay: for whatsoever is more than these cometh of evil"

Matthew 5:37

"But there were false prophets also among the people, even as there shall be false teachers among you, who privily shall bring in damnable heresies, even denying the Lord that bought them and bring upon themselves swift destruction. And shall follow their pernicious ways; by reason of whom the truth shall be evil spoken of"

2 Peter 2: 1-2

"They say, if a man put away his wife, and she go from him, and become another man's, shall he return unto her again? Shall not that land be greatly polluted? But thou hast played the harlot with many lovers, yet return again to me, saith the Lord"

Revelation 22:18-19

1. Introduction:

Compromise is commonly used in, <u>political, labor</u> marital, and parental disputes. Compromise involves conceding, concessions, a sacrifice of principles, fitting in, being politically correct, and more. It can also involve the partial surrender of one's position in concession to another party. It is a delicate balance between blessing and judgment, good and evil, truth and lie, correct and wrong, and complete obedience and partial obedience. When you compromise, you are all over the place and end up kissing up everything to please everyone. Compromising is like harlotry when a woman has many lovers. Today, an average person feels that all religion is good as long as one is sincere. It is only by uncompromising faith that we can prove otherwise. Generally, people prefer compromise—a little bit of religion, a little bit of the world, and sin. While God wants us not to compromise, Satan wants us to compromise for a watered-down religion and mediocre Christianity. Compromise is the erosion of our good intentions through progressive rationalization. Compromise can come about when individuals settle their differences by mutual concessions. While it may be helpful in conflict resolutions involving human relations, God hates compromise when it comes to His will. God demands absolute obedience from His children. For example, disobeying God does not reverence Him before His children. Disobeying God's instructions compromises His word. The consequences of defying God's authority are ugly (***Hebrews 12:29).***

Uncompromising faith is a spiritual revolution in which people find freedom through Jesus, not religion, and spend time convincing others to refuse to accept the status quo and instead to bring compassion and honesty back to the church. With the love of many becoming cold, we have to practice compassion without compromise. For example, we have to love people whose lifestyles are at variance with the word of God but tell them in a loving way that the word of God does not approve of their lifestyles.

In a true church, worship requires true dedication, an uncompromising faith, and separation from sin. For example, after conversion, we expect to smash the liquor bottles, flush the drugs, burn the paraphernalia, throw the old reggae or rock and roll music to make room for the new, burn the porn, dump it out of your computer. Borderline (lukewarm) Christians follow Christ and then return to the world. Satan loves borderline Christians because they are neither cold nor warm, and he has them under his belt.

The Lord of the church will not accept any form of tolerance in His church that compromises His truth. In the perfect church of the Lord, false teaching is not tolerated. When we compromise, we look so much like the world that it becomes difficult to tell any difference between us. The cure for tolerance of sin is repentance. Repentance involves a change of mind, changing one's lifestyle, and rerouting your life. If you are tolerating sinful practices in your secret personal life, you are compromising your faith and salvation. You cannot tolerate sin and please the Lord Jesus Christ at the same time. You cannot serve two masters (Satan and Jesus Christ). The consequence of compromising and not repenting is to incur the displeasure of Jesus Christ. If you do not repent, Jesus Christ Himself will come to fight against you with His word. The church of Jesus Christ is continually compromising the word of God to the extent that if the Lord's Second coming is delayed, few souls can be saved.

The reason why many compromise their faith and salvation is that they do not trust Jesus Christ. The failure of repentance will keep you compromising and incur the wrath and judgment of God. It is a fearful thing to fall into the hands of the living God *(Hebrews 10:31)*. When we compromise God's word and ways, we put ourselves in bondage to Satan and the world. However, total commitment to Jesus Christ leaves no room for compromise. We need to allow Christ to be the Lord of our entire lives. The degree of compromising God's truth in this present age is not different from the compromises we read in the past.

2. Biblical Examples and Effects of those who compromised

Abram compromised the truth by traveling past Canaan unto Egypt and lying to the Egyptians that Sarai was her sister.

> ***"And Abram journeyed, going on still toward the South. And there was a famine in the land: and Abram went down into Egypt to sojourn there, for the famine was grievous in the land. And it came to pass, when he was come near to enter into Egypt, that he said into Sarai his wife, Behold now, I know that thou art a fair woman to like upon. Therefore, it shall come to pass, when the Egyptians shall see thee that they will kill me, but they will save thee alive. Say, I pray thee, thou art my sister: that it may be well with me for thy sake; and my soul shall live because of thee"***

> ***Genesis 12: 9-13***

Abram knew that God intended for him to go to Canaan and be blessed there. But he eyed at Egypt. He compromised when he passed through Canaan because of the giants. Again, Abram compromised his wife's safety to preserve his own safety. By ending up in Egypt, he forsook God's perfect will and delayed his blessing. Arguably, Abram left Egypt with goodies that Pharaoh had given them. Nobody can out-give God. God wanted to make him a father of many nations in Canaan, but he passed through and kept on going. God wanted to use him to take the demons out of the land and the devil along with them, but he passed by them and kept them ongoing. Another remarkable event in Abram's journey to Egypt was that he did not build an altar and pitch a tent in Egypt. This means Abram did not commune with God and did not separate himself from the world around him. In order to be in God's perfect will, Abram had to go back to the place where he last heard God.

God is waiting for you and me to be back to where we left Him, commune, and repent of compromising His truth and instructions. Pitch your tent and separate yourself from the world and unto God.

The Israelites compromised the commandment of God by having many idols to incur the displeasure of God.

> ***"Thou shalt not bow down thyself unto them, nor serve them: for I the Lord thy God am a jealous God, visiting the iniquity of the fathers upon the children unto the third and fourth generation of them that hate me"***

> ***Deuteronomy 5:9***

Compromising the word of God by turning aside to serve other gods provokes God and has a long-lasting evil consequence on generations. God is a consuming fire and a jealous God. Today, many people, particularly Christians, have agendas that supersede God's plan. God is either ahead of our agendas or never. Today, Christians have replaced God's agenda with their activities but they are still not happy.

Samson was the promised son to Manoah, a Nazarite who was expected to deliver Israel out of the hand of the Philistines.

> ***"For, lo, thou shall conceive and bear a son; and no razor shall come on his head, for the***

> **child shall be a Nazarite unto God from the
> womb; and he shall begin to deliver Israel out
> of the hand of the Philistines"**

> **Judges 13:5**

Samson performed wonders with the Spirit of the Lord that rested upon him. The Philistines hated him and used one of their own Delilah to bring Samson down. Samson compromised the instructions of God by telling the secret of his strength to Delilah. This almost cost him his salvation.

> **"But the Philistines took him, and put out his
> eyes, and brought him down to Gaza, and bound
> him with fetters of brass, and he did grind in the
> prison house. And Samson said; let me die with
> the Philistines. And he bowed himself with all
> his might, and the house fell upon the Lords,
> and upon all the people that were therein. So
> the dead which he slew at his death were more
> than they which he slew in his life"**

> **Judges 16:21, 30**

Today, many Christians are not learning from Samson's account. They continue to be unequally yoked with unbelievers. Compromising your marriage, friendship will have long-term devastating consequences on your faith and salvation. Many Christians are marrying unbelievers who are Muslim, Buddhist, Pseudo-Christians, and more. This unholy alliance will not take you to heaven. God hates such alliances.

By disobeying and compromising God's instructions, Saul lost his throne to David. Because he rejected and compromised the word of the Lord, God rejected him from being king of Israel.

> *"Because thou obeyedst not the voice of the Lord, nor executedst his fierce wrath upon Amalek, therefore hath the Lord done this thing unto thee this day"*
>
> *1 Samuel 28:18*

In addition, the Lord delivered Israel into the hand of the Philistines. Therefore, by one man's disobedience and compromise, many people faced the wrath of God. Today, many leaders and statesmen are compromising the truth and bringing untold hardships to many innocent people.

When the young prophet in the book of first Kings compromised his faith and disobeyed the word of the Lord, it cost him his life and salvation. The man of God who had performed a miracle by restoring the withered hand of king Jeroboam lost his life when he compromised the word of the Lord. One lesson to be learned here is, trust no man but the Lord *(Jeremiah 17:7)*. The young prophet thought he was with another man of God and could not go wrong. Not everyone who calls himself/herself a Christian is a true Christian. Many are working for Satan to trap and deceive Christians into hell. Listen to how the old prophet cajoled the young prophet to his death:

"For it was said to me by the word of the Lord, Thou shalt eat no bread nor drink water there, nor turn again to go by the way that thou camest. He said unto him, I am a prophet also as thou art; and an angel spake unto me by the word of the Lord, saying, Bring him back with thee into thine house, that he may eat bread and drink water. But he lied unto him. So he went back with him, and did eat bread in his house, and drank water. And it came to pass, as they sat at the table, that the word of the Lord came unto the prophet that brought him back; And he cried unto the man of God that came from Judah, saying, Thus, saith the Lord, Forasmuch as thou hast disobeyed the mouth of the Lord, and hast not kept the commandment which the Lord thy God commanded thee"

1 Kings 13:17-21

The young prophet was in the counsel of the ungodly. Remember, not all churchgoers are Christians. At the same time, not all Christians are real. There are many tares among the wheat so trust no one.

Demas left Paul. He compromised with the world system because he loved all that was in the world. He chose the present world over eternity.

"For Demas hath forsaken me, having loved the present world, and is departed unto

Thessalonica; Crescens to Galatia, Titus unto Dalmatia"

2 Timothy 4: 10

Today, there are many "Demases" in the churches of the Lord who are compromising the word of God by deceiving many in the church and accepting all the things of the world. If you are a friend to the world, you are the enemy of God.

When Ananias and his wife Sapphira lied to the Holy Spirit and God on the proceeds of their land sale, it cost them their lives. They thought they could get away with deceiving Peter and compromising the truth of the word God by declaring a part of the proceeds.

> *"But Peter said, Ananias, as to why hath Satan filled thine heart to lie to the Holy Ghost and to keep back part of the price of the land. Whiles it remained, was it not thine own? And after it was sold, was it not in thine own power? Why hast thou conceived this thing in thine heart? Thou hast not lied unto men, but unto God. And Ananias as hearing these words fell down and gave up the ghost, and great fear came on all them that heard these things"*

Acts 5:3-5

You cannot compromise the truth of God and go scot-free It will cost you your faith, eternal salvation, and even your life.

3. Biblical Examples and Effects of those who refused to Compromise

Enoch walked with God and never compromised God's words. He did not see physical death because God took him away to heaven.

> ***"And Enoch walked with God: and he was not;***
> ***for God took him"***

> ***Genesis 5: 24***

Noah did not compromise the truth and God used his household to save the world.

> ***But with thee will I establish my covenant; and***
> ***thou shalt come into the ark, thou, and thy sons,***
> ***and thy wife, and thy sons' wives with thee"***

> ***Genesis 6: 18***

Noah did all that God commanded him to do and never compromised God's truth. Building an ark would have made no sense to him but followed the instructions.

Joseph refused to lie with his master's wife when he had the chance.

> ***"But he refused, and said unto his master's***
> ***wife, Behold, my master' wotteth not what is***
> ***with me in the house, and he hath committed***
> ***all that he hath to my hand; There is none***
> ***greater in this house than I; neither hath he***

*kept back anything from me but thee, because
thou art his wife: how then can I do this great
wickedness and sin against God?"*

Genesis 39: 8-9

When his master's wife caught him by his garment asking
him to lie with her, Joseph fled and got out. Paul warned us
to flee from fornication and not compromise.

*"Flee fornication. Every sin that a man doeth
is without the body; but he that committeth
fornication sinneth against his own body.
What? Know ye not that your body is the temple
of the Holy Ghost which is in you, which ye have
of God, and ye are not your own? For ye are
bought with a price: therefore glorify God in
your body, and in your spirit, which are God's"*

1 Corinthians 6: 18-20

Historically, many great men of God have been brought
down to their knees by women as God's words and ways are
compromised. As I write, many continue to fall to the old
tricks of having affair with wrong women.

Moses could have chosen to become the king of Egypt, but
he gave it up to lead his people through the wilderness.

Joshua did not compromise with Satan when his family
was involved. The enemy and his demons want more than

anything to have our families in his possession. But our families are to serve God with us.

> ***"And if it seems evil unto you to serve the Lord, choose you this day whom ye will serve; whether the gods which your fathers served on the other side of the flood or the gods of the Amorites, in whose land ye dwell: but as for me and my house, we will that were serve the Lord"***

> ***Joshua 24:15***

All of us had and have opportunities to compromise our faith, family, and possessions. We have taken a stand against the world and Satan that "As for me and my house we will serve the Lord" Satan does not want God to have you, your family, and your possessions. Today many families have been torn apart by Satan through compromises. Do not compromise for anything with Satan.

Jesus faced the crucifixion without compromise. His father could have changed death by crucifixion for him.

> ***"And he went forward a little, and fell on the ground, and prayed that, if it were possible, the hour might pass from him. And he said, Abba, Father, all things are possible unto thee; take away this cup from me; nevertheless, not what I will, but what thou wilt"***

> ***Mark 14: 35-36***

Jesus could have compromised his death on the cross to save mankind but allowed the Father's will to prevail. He could have called twelve legions to defend him. He is our prime example of not compromising for anything with Satan.

All the apostles did not compromise with the word of truth, and all were martyred. It is feasible to believe that all but one of the apostles suffered a martyr's death. Amidst some uncertainty, one thing is clear—the reason given for their deaths was the same. They were killed because they claimed to be eyewitnesses of Christ's death and resurrection. They all died because of an unwavering, unrelenting claim that Christ rose from the grave. Stephen was the first to be martyred. James, the apostle of the Lord, was the second recorded martyr after Christ's death. Although Peter denied Christ three times just before the crucifixion, after the resurrection, he was willing to be martyred for his belief. He was crucified headlong. Andrew, who introduced his brother Peter to Christ, was martyred six years after Peter. Thomas sealed his testimony as he was thrust through with pine spears, tormented with red-hot plates, and burned alive. Philip saw the glory of Christ after the resurrection and was undoubtedly amazed at Christ's response to his request. Philip evangelized in Phrygia, where hostile Jews had him tortured and then crucified. Matthew, the tax collector, desperately wanted the Jews to accept Christ. He was beheaded at Nad-Davar. Nathanael, whose name means "gift of God", was truly given as a gift to the Church through his martyrdom. James was the appointed head of the Jerusalem church for many years after Christ's death. James was cast down from the Temple and finally beaten to death with a fuller's club to the head. Simon was a Jewish zealot who strived to set his people free from Roman oppression. After he saw with his own eyes that Christ had been resurrected, he became a zealot of the Gospel. His martyrdom, brought about by a governor in Syria, verified his testimony for Christ. After he witnessed Christ's resurrection, Judas Thaddeus knew the answer. He preached the risen Christ in the midst of pagan priests in Mesopotamia. He was eventually beaten to death with sticks, showing to the world that Christ was indeed Lord and God. Matthias replaced Judas Iscariot (the betrayer of Christ who hanged himself) as the twelfth apostle of Christ. Matthias preached in Ethiopia. He was later stoned while hanging upon a cross. John is the only one of the twelve apostles who died a natural death. Although he did not die a martyr's death, he did live a martyr's life. He was exiled to the Island of Patmos during the reign of Emperor Domitian for his proclamation of the risen Christ. Some traditions say he was thrown into boiling oil before the Latin Gate. While this didn't kill him, it likely scarred him for life. Paul was brought to repentance as he traveled to Damascus. Ironically, he was on his way to arrest those who held to Jesus' resurrection. Paul started as the greatest skeptic but spent the rest of his life proclaiming the Christ he once persecuted. Paul met his death at the hands of Emperor Nero when he was beheaded in Rome.

People do not die for their own lies, half-truths, or fabrications. The apostles' deaths increase our confidence in the resurrection of our Lord Jesus Christ. Many died (are dying) for something they knew (know) to be a lie. Modern-day Christians are afraid of persecutions, longsuffering, and even martyrdom. They are interested in praising, worshipping, and dancing. They cannot die for the Lord as the Lord died for them.

Writing in 2 Corinthians 11:23–27, defending his ministry, Paul tells of his sufferings for the name of Christ.

> *"Are they ministers of Christs? (I speak as a fool) I am more; in labours more abundant, in stripes above measure, in prisons more frequent, in deaths oft. Of the Jews, five times received I forty stripes save one. Thrice was I beaten with rods, once was I stoned, thrice I suffered shipwreck, a night and a day I have been in the deep; In journeyings often, in perils in the city, in perils of robbers, in perils in the city, in perils in the wilderness, in perils in the sea, in perils among false brethren; In weariness and painfulness, in watchings often, in hunger and thirst, in fastings often, in cold and nakedness"*

If you do not have the hard experiences of the apostles, particularly Paul, Peter, and Jesus Christ Himself, the probability of you compromising the truth of God is very high. John, the Baptist, was beheaded during Jesus Christ's ministry on earth. Many confessed Christians will chicken out (compromise) when the martyrdom of Jesus Christ is on the line. We need to get the word of God in our system, particularly what Paul taught us in the book of Romans 8: 35-39.

> *"Who shall separate us from the love of Christ? Shall tribulation or distress, or persecution, or famine, nakedness, or peril, or sword? As it is written, for thy sake, we are killed all the day long; we are accounted as sheep for the slaughter. Nay, in all these things we are more*

> ***than conquerors through him that loved us. For
> I am persuaded, that neither death, nor life,
> nor angels, nor principalities, nor powers, nor
> things present, nor things to come. Nor height,
> nor depth, nor any other creature, shall be able
> to separate us from the love of God, which is in
> Christ Jesus Our Lord"***

4. Get Real with the Word of God.

The degree of compromising God's truth in this present age
is not different from the compromises in the past. The only
difference is that increased knowledge in technology makes
it look like this era is an age of compromises.

Do not compromise your faith for money, marriage, health,
or anything. For example, your heart tells you the person
you are about to marry is wrong, but your need is stronger.
It is good to marry, but do not let the desire for marriage
compromise your faith. There are no marriages in heaven.
Proverbs warns us that *"It is better to dwell in the wilderness
than with a contentious and an angry woman"* Proverbs 21:19.
Every Christian will one day, fight for different causes. Each
one of us (true Christians) will suffer for Christ. Fight a good
fight of faith and remain faithful to the end as the apostles did.

The downward trend away from biblical Christianity should
alarm every true Christ-follower. The fact that many so-called
Christian seminaries eventually digressed away from their
original fidelity to Scripture and evolved into propagating a
form of universalism (the belief that Jesus saved every human

on the cross, irrespective of whether they believe in Him or not) and pluralism (that there are many roads to God not just through Jesus) beginning since the early days of Harvard and Yale divinity schools (to appease and accommodate the prevailing intellectual climate and culture) is one of the root causes of this growing rot in mainline churches.

If a pastor rarely preaches biblically sound messages from a text of Scripture and merely relies on oratory skill or rhetoric, which excites the emotion but fails to holistically feed the soul, then the said church has sand as its foundation *(Matthew. 7:24-27).* Such a preacher has an emotionally alive church that lacks biblical discernment *(Hebrews. 5:12-14),* which can easily lead members down the road to pluralism or universalism if the pastor so desires.

Finally, Jesus warned His followers about following false prophets *(Matthew. 7:15),* as did the apostle Peter when he predicted that false teachers would arise that will secretly introduce destructive heresies and that many will follow them. Because of them, the way of truth will be maligned *(2 Peter. 2:1, 2).*

The long list of the more obvious heretics/false teachers to be marked & avoided will surprise you. Many of them come from Africa and North America.

Jesus, apostles Paul, Peter, and John all repeatedly warned such men would rise up among us and lead many astray, even within the visible church. They warned that not only would there be many False Teachers, but there would also be many followers of them as well ...people "to suit their own desires ...will gather around them a great number of teachers to say what their itching ears want to hear." *(2 Timothy 4:3).* Sadly, very few people do their homework when considering their own pastors, so the wolves have taken advantage of this fact to keep multitudes in their blinded condition. Obviously, we should not easily call other people a heretic, but if they publicly teach doctrine long recognized by the church as false, then we ought to call it out.

All the seven churches listed in Revelation 1:11 *(Ephesus, Smyrna, Pergamum, Thyatira, Sardis, Philadelphia, and Laodicea)* compromised the truth of God by allowing lasciviousness among them, devil worship, worldly practices, Jezebel spirit, anything-goes spirit, feels-good spirit, adultery, lying spirit, and few more. The Lord recommends the church and us to double down our commitment to Him and deny Satan and the world by repenting of our sins.

Politicians are compromising every time to get elected. Pastors and other workmen of God are compromising every day to find favor with men than God. Judges are compromising all the time on the law to get favors from their clients. Everybody is compromising one way or another to fit in or satisfy a peer group.

Today, we are taught that we can take the music, fads, and fashion of the world and mix it with biblical truths and that will make us Christians. This is the doctrine of Balaam. It is the teaching that God's people can mix with the world while maintaining their Christian distinctiveness and it is widespread in our churches today. Do not compromise your faith and church. The world is corrupting Christianity.

5. Final Thoughts

In truth, none of the sufferings of the apostles were in vain, for the Lord Jesus Christ was crucified by the ungodly.

A confrontation may be too uncomfortable for some. Calling someone a heretic may seem too judgmental.   Many simply follow the crowd rather than follow the Bible unwilling and unequipped to challenge the faith they were raised in. Maybe it is too difficult to think this deeply, but Jesus said, "the way is easy that leads to destruction, but it is the difficult narrow path that leads to life". Christians must, therefore, arm themselves against false prophets and recognize who they are required to acknowledge. But, knowledge requires a study of God's word.

- Heresy is to "preach another gospel", as Paul stated in Galatians 1:9.

- Technically, speaking something is not a heresy just because the church deemed it so. It is heretical because it is teaching which has abandoned the "pattern of sound teaching."

Christ calls us to have a complete commitment to Him. Total commitment means at times, we will be unhappy for a season, but the Lord is with us. The type of commitment is in (***Romans 12: 1-2).*** We also need to say I am not going to compromise with you, Satan, when it comes to my family. Satan wants more than anything to have our families in his possession. Remember, we are to serve God with our families.

How do you want to finish your faith race? Fight a good fight of faith looking at Jesus Christ in heaven. Do not compromise on anything in your life. The consequences of your compromising behavior can even cost you your salvation.

If we are totally committed to the Lord, we will not walk in the counsel of the ungodly by looking at pornography and lust. One compromise, then two, then three, will make it harder and harder to walk away from the counsel of the ungodly *(Psalm 1:1)*. Again, if we are totally committed to the Lord, we will not stand in the way of sinners by getting involved in their sinful lifestyles *(Psalm 1:1)*.

Finally, if we are fully committed to the Lord, we will not sit in the seat of scoffers by turning aside to sin *(Psalm 1:1)*.

There is a time to refuse to bow when God's truth directs us to conflict with the prevailing culture around us. When we refuse to bow as, in the case of Daniel and his three Hebrew friends, we have to be prepared to get burned But don't worry when things get tough, the Lord Himself will show up in the furnace..

When the handwriting is on the wall, and we know where our culture is headed, it is time to be prophetic in people's lives by sharing grace and truth with the loving heart of Jesus Christ.

Do not compromise on anything because small compromises lead to big ones. One small compromise by King David led him to big compromises (2 Samuel 11). At the time that kings went off to war, David stayed behind in Jerusalem doing what? This was the first compromise. He watched a naked woman from the roof of his palace and lusted for Bathsheba. This was his second compromise (2 Samuel 11:2). He later committed adultery with her and resulted in pregnancy. This was his third compromise (2 Samuel 11: 3-4). Then, when David could not contain his shame, he killed her husband by putting him in front of the war. This was his fourth compromise (2 Samuel 11:14-24). From neglect to lust, to adultery to murder, David drifted away from God into moral chaos. Now, if it happened to King David, a man after God's own heart, then it can happen to you and me. Thus, compromise devastates the people of God.

Also, Ziglag was another place for David's compromise. David's fear led him to depression. He determined to hide from Saul in the land of Philistines. David decided to seek favor with the enemies of God, Philistines, instead of God. He said:

> *"I shall now perish one day by the hand of Saul: there is nothing better than that, I should speedily escape into the land of Philistines; and Saul shall despair of me, to seek me anymore in any coast of Israel: so shall I escape out of his land".*
>
> *1 Samuel 27:1*

God loved David so much that He allowed the place of his compromise to be burned. Sometimes we live in compromise because we are afraid that God will not deliver us. Thus, we plan for a way to deliver ourselves. We hide in a Ziglag of our own making. Eventually, God will burn our Ziglag, and remove all the props we falsely trust. Fear makes us compromise and trust in people and things that cannot give us permanent assurance and security.

The long-term cost of compromising is far greater than non-compromising. Stand up for the truth, despite all odds. Buy-in for the cross and the blood of Jesus and do not sell them out

6. Let's Pray

Like Jonah, Lord, help me *[insert your name about here]* to stop running, compromising, and turn to you. Keep me from spiritual blindness and compromising spirit in the age of compromise. Lord, help me *[insert your name about here]* not to be politically correct to accept and trust anyone who is sincere regardless of their beliefs. Father, let not Satan, who controls this world hide the truth of the gospel from me. Satan, in the name of Jesus' you cannot crush me *[insert your name about here]* with hardship and hostility or corrupt me with compromise. Holy Spirit, transform me by renewing my mind 24/7.

Lord, let the eyes of my understanding be enlightened not to compromise your truth in Jesus' name. O Lord, perfect what is lacking in my faith. Oh God, help me to comprehend the breadth, length, depth, and height of the love of Christ in the name of Jesus. May the Holy Spirit open my heart and eyes to the light of the Kingdom of God.

I *[insert your name about here]* am the sincere Christ-follower who searches the Scriptures daily and be more shaped by the Word of God than the words of any man apart from Jesus Christ. Lord Jesus, help me to learn and walk in the fullness of my purpose and destiny by living each day with Holy Spirit. May the Lord cause my faith not to fail. Father, let me *[insert your name about here]* live for Christ and in Him only.

Let the eyes of my understanding be enlightened that I might know the hope of my calling, the riches of the glory of your inheritance in the saints, and the exceeding greatness of your power toward me, who believes *(Ephesians 1:17-19)*. Strengthen me with might by your Spirit in the inner man *(Ephesians 3:16)*. Let Christ dwell in my heart by faith, let me be rooted and grounded in love, and let me comprehend with all saints the breadth and length and depth height of your love *(Ephesians 3:17-18)*. Let utterance be given unto me that I may open my mouth boldly to make known the mystery of the Gospel *(Ephesians 6:19)*. Let me, *[insert your name about here]*, know Jesus and the power of his resurrection and the fellowship of his sufferings, being made conformable unto his death *(Philippians 3:10)*. Let me be filled with the knowledge of your will in all wisdom and spiritual understanding that I might walk worthy of you unto all pleasing, being fruitful in every good work, and increasing in the knowledge of God *(Colossians 1: 9-10)*. Let me be strengthened with all might according to Your glorious power unto all patience and long-suffering with joyfulness *(Colossians 1:11).* Let me, *[insert your name about here],* stand perfect and complete in the will of God *(Colossians 4:12).* Father, let my whole spirit and soul and body be preserved blameless unto the coming of my Lord Jesus Christ *(1 Thessalonians 5:23).* Lord, give me peace always by all means and be with me *(2 Thessalonians 3:16).*

I, *[insert your name about here],* make supplication, intercession, and give thanks for all men and leaders in my nation and in the church that I might lead a quiet and peaceable life in all godliness and honesty *(1 Timothy 2:1-2).* I receive multiplied grace and peace through the apostolic anointing *(2 Peter 1:2).*

I live for Christ regardless of this present environment. I *[insert your name about here]* do not bow to any other false gods and the world systems around me. Lord, help me to reject the friendship of the world and enjoy the unique friendship with you.

Jesus Christ defeated the whole kingdom of darkness and won an overwhelming victory by disarming principalities and powers at the cross. Jesus is the victor. He is a mighty conqueror. Jesus triumphed over all his foes, and he has given me complete victory over every foe in my life. This includes a victory over Satan, demons, and the whole kingdom of darkness, as well as victory over all works of darkness, including witches and wizards. Therefore, Satan, demons, witches, and warlocks, you have absolutely no power and no authority over me. Lord Jesus, let your kingdom come in the power of the Holy Spirit and glory of God. I *[insert your name about here]* seal this prayer with the precious blood of the Great Shepherd of the sheep and with thanksgiving. Amen.

97

Chapter 4

You must be born again to keep your ticket to Heaven

"And the earth was without form, and void; and darkness was upon the face of the deep. And the Spirit of God moved upon the face of the waters"

Genesis 1:2

"And Moses made a serpent of brass, and put it upon a pole; and it came to pass, that if a serpent had bitten any man, when he beheld the serpent of brass, he lived"

Numbers 21:9

"Jesus answered and said unto him, verily, verily I say unto thee, except a man be born again, he cannot see the kingdom of God; &
"That which is born of the flesh; and that which is born of the Spirit is spirit"

John 3:3; 6

"The wind bloweth where it listeth, and thou hearest the sound thereof, but canst not tell whence it cometh, and whither. It goeth; so is every one that is born of the Spirit"

John 3:8

"But when the Comforter is come, whom I will send unto you from the Father, even the Spirit of truth, which proceedeth from the Father, he shall testify of me"

John 15:26

"Ye are of God, little children, and have overcome them: because greater is he that is in you, than he that is in the world"

1 John 4:4

"Jesus saith unto him, I am the way, the truth, and the life, no man cometh unto the Father, but by me"

John 14:6

"Not by works of righteousness which we have done, but according to his mercy he saved us, by the washing of regeneration, and renewing of the Holy Ghost; which he shed on us abundantly through Jesus Christ our Savior; That being justified by his grace, we should be made heirs according to the hope of eternal life"

Titus 3:5-7

1. Introduction:

Life choices do not come cheap, and they come with temporal and eternal consequences. Some are made as spur-of-the-moment and can have lasting consequences. Others are made after long and critical reviews, and they also have consequences. Don't be deceived, and you cannot mock God, so whatever a man sows, he shall also reap (Galatians 6:7). As Christians, the most sacred choice we make is about eternal life. How do you obtain eternal life? In order words, the most important theme in the past, now, and the future of Christianity is "You must be born again to enter heaven". What is born again? How can you obtain Born Again (BA) degree? This is why Jesus Christ confronted Nicodemus, a Jewish religious philosopher, with the statement, "You must be born again. To apostle Paul born again means, all Christians must present their bodies as living sacrifices, holy and acceptable unto God, and be not conformed to this world but be ye transformed by renewing of minds (Romans 12:1-2). Apostle John's contribution to being born again is "Love not the world, neither the things that are in the world. For all that is in the world, the lust of the flesh, and the lust of the eyes, and the pride of life, is not of the Father but is of the world (1 John 2:15-16). Peter refers to being born again as "Purified souls obeying the truth through the Spirit unto unfeigned love. Loving one another with pure hearts. Being born again, not of corruptible seed, but of incorruptible, by the word of God, which liveth and abideth forever: (1 Peter 1: 22-23). John Wesley spent the greater part of his sermons on "You must be born again" Jesus also emphasized "born Again" as the key requirement to go to heaven. Everybody should be preaching on getting "Born Again" Being born again is taking the likeness of Jesus and holding on to your heaven ticket to eternity.

2. *Personality of the Holy Spirit*

There is so much misconception on the identity of the Holy Spirit that many Christians think He is an impersonal healing or protective power which God makes available to Christians who want Him all. However, the Bible makes it clear that Holy Spirit is a person —the third person of the Trinity. In fact, the Holy Spirit is God. He is a divine person who is our comforter and a counselor, according to the promise of Jesus Christ **(John 14: 16, 26; 15:26).** The Holy Spirit is intimately involved in our salvation, accompanied by the Father and the Son.

> *"But if the Spirit of him that raised up Jesus from the dead dwell in you, he that raised up Christ from the dead shall also quicken your mortal bodies by his Spirit that dwelleth in you"*
>
> *Romans 8:11*

Holy Spirit has thoughts and knowledge (1 Corinthians 2:10). Furthermore, Holy Spirit can make intercession for believers **(Romans 8:26-27)** and also has a will and makes decisions (1 Corinthians 12:7-11). He can feel sorrow and grief **(Ephesians 4:30).** Most importantly, Holy Spirit is a gentleman and will not force His will on you. Similarly, God has the power to make everybody worship Him, but He will not force us to obey Him.

Holy Spirit is as vital to the life of a Christian as AIR we breathe, and without Him we will struggle with our walk with God and Jesus. He is the invisible third person of the Trinity who shares equal power with the Father and Jesus Christ. Holy Spirit is the Spirit of truth. The secular world cannot accept Him because it neither sees Him nor knows Him. Holy Spirit lives inside every believer, and He can be either active or dormant in a believer's life. The bible's teaching on the Holy Spirit is clear, but many Christians remain ignorant on this subject. Most Christians have high clarity of understanding God the Father and His Son Jesus Christ, but their understanding of the Holy Spirit is vague and murky. Thus, of the three Persons of the Godhead — Father, Son, and Holy Spirit — Holy Spirit seems to be the least known and understood by today's Christians. Honestly, He is most greatly and intimately involved in our initial conversion and birth into the family of God and the ongoing activities of our Christian lives. Our intimate relationship with the Holy Spirit brings joy, power, and hope, as well as other fruits of the Spirit to our lives. Holy Spirit is our spiritual thermometer who instructs and directs us in decisions and paths we choose.

In summary, the Holy Spirit is God Himself. He is the third person of the Trinity. As a divine person, the Holy Spirit is a true comforter and a counselor for believers according to the promise of Jesus *(John 14:16, 26; John 15:26).*

3. Why little knowledge or ignorance on the Holy Spirit?

Negligence, ignorance, or indifference of the Holy Spirit has brought spiritual drought in the lives of many Christians. The reasons for this spiritual wilderness are as follows:

First, the Holy Spirit doctrine is not easy to grasp by many Christians, so many just avoid it together. Our new generation wants everything simple and straightforward and avoids complex truth.

Second, an average Christian has placed Holy Spirit THIRD in the Trinity — Father, first; Son, second, and Holy Spirit in their in the Trinity — Father, first; Son, second, and Holy Spirit in their minds. This ranking order has unnecessarily relegated the Holy Spirit to an unimportant position. God created the universe by His Holy Spirit, so He is as powerful as God.

Third, many believers knowingly or unknowingly think of the Holy Spirit as non-person and an impersonal influence. We have done a great job of dispelling this misconception. Extant texts in the Scriptures indicate that the Holy Spirit is a person. Jesus referred to the Holy Spirit as HIM [**John 14:17; John 14:26; John 15:26; John 16:13 and John 16: 14-15**]. The Holy Spirit testifies, comforts, reproves, helps, guides, and enables believers.

> *"Likewise the Spirit also helpeth our infirmities for we know not what we should pray for as we ought: but the Spirit itself maketh intercession for us with groanings which cannot be uttered.*

> **And he that searcheth the hearts knoweth what the mind of the Spirit is because he maketh intercession for the saints according to the will of God"**
>
> **Romans 8: 26-27**

The person of the Holy Spirit distributes spiritual gifts (1 Corinthians 12:7-11) to each one, just as He determines who gets what. Holy Spirit can be quenched or stifled. Thus, one can say to the Holy Spirit, be quiet, leave me alone, and stop talking to me. If you have done that, then you are grieving the person of the Holy Spirit. The person of the Holy Spirit is divine majesty and glory who gets hold of you gently and uses you to bring glory to God.

Finally, believers are afraid of the emotional excesses of many who embrace false teachings about the Holy Spirit. The overboard excesses of many Christians who are under the influence of the Holy Spirit can be confusing for both young and old believers. For example, false pretenses of barking like dogs, and uncontrollable laughter in a church setting, can scare many young and immature Christians. Bad rap and false teachings on the Holy Spirit have caused many sincere believers to steer away from the person of the Holy Spirit.

The good news is that Holy Spirit is a PERSON and does things like us. He has feelings and gets withdrawn from us if we hurt him with our negative attitude. He is a gentleman and will not resist us if He is not welcome. Also, Holy Spirit is God Himself because he possesses attributes that belong only to God. For instance, Holy Spirit is ETERNAL (*Hebrews 9:14*). And is also OMNIPRESENT. The Holy Spirit does work that only God can do (*Psalm 139:7*). He was involved in the creation.

"The Spirit of God moved upon the waters"

Genesis 1:2

He is involved in the new birth we experience when we become Christians (Born-again)

The wind bloweth where it listeth, and thou hearest the sound thereof, but canst not tell whence it cometh, and whither it goeth: so is every one that is born of the Spirit"

John 3:8

Holy Spirit is co-equal and co-eternal with the FATHER and the SON. The Holy Spirit is as much God as is the SON, or the FATHER is. He is distinct from God, yet essentially one with God. Many churches stray away from the Holy Spirit because of the Holy TRINITY. God is ONE, God is not THREE, God is not TWO, but ONE. The Lord, Our God is One Lord (*Deuteronomy 6:4*). We must understand that Jesus is not a Second God..., not just one-third of God. In fact, Jesus is the eternal God uniquely present in truly human life. Similarly, the Holy Spirit is neither a Third God nor one-Third of God. Holy Spirit is God Himself in His nearness and power, anywhere and anytime. Thus, divine presence incarnated in Jesus Christ is now present in His people. Thus, the Holy Spirit in Christians is Jesus Christ in them.

All believers must be aware that God is not only with us, but He (the Holy Spirit) is in us. Holy Spirit is indeed an ever Present Holy Resident in the lives of all believers. No matter where you are if you are a Christian, God is there in you. Besides, He is always ready to help. He works 24/7 for all believers. Holy Spirit inside a believer gives him/her power, guidance, comfort, and whatever it is He knows that you need.

Holy Spirit gives a believer instant access to all the power he/she needs to work. With respect to the Holy Spirit, God chooses to be a power-sharing God. He cares very much about us to impart us with His strength when we need it to live as He wants us to live. For example, the Holy Spirit enables us to say "NO" to temptation and say "Yes" to the truth. He empowers us to do His will and more exceedingly. Note that the very power that raised Jesus Christ from the Dead is available to us as Christians through the indwelling Holy Spirit of God. Holy Spirit limitless capabilities are resident within us and enable us to do exploit. With our world spinning out of control, coupled with moral decay, high divorce rates, addictions, diverse diseases, and health-related complications, the demand for professional counselors, social workers, diviners, sorcerers, prophets (including false prophets), and related professionals is on the rise. Why? The world hates spiritual answers for secular problems.

Holy Spirit has all the answers to all these problems. Holy Spirit is more than qualified to counsel or guide and counsel us in every area of life. Prophet Isaiah put it this way. The Lord of hosts is a wonderful counsel and excellent in guidance *(Isaiah 28:29).* Believers can hear the small little voice of the Holy Spirit as He guides and counsels us in many circumstances. For instance, He tells believers How to Pray because we do not know what we ought to pray for, but the Spirit Himself intercedes for us with groans that words cannot express *(Romans 8:26).*

> *"However, people without Holy Spirit do not accept the things that come from God, for they are foolishness to them and He cannot understand them, because they are spiritually discerned"*
>
> *1 Corinthians 2:14.*

Many believers live in the false hope of being born again because they have not met Jesus face-to-face in the wilderness. Like Nicodemus, they are regular churchgoers, pay their tithes and offering, hold high positions in the church, are excellent workmen of God; they have not experienced the full power of the Holy Spirit in their lives.

4. How to receive and Keep your Heaven ticket (Holy Spirit)

There are many ways that the Holy Spirit works in the lives of Christians, but they all come to one common goal — making believers in the image of Jesus Christ. The seal of the Holy Spirit takes place at the point of salvation. We receive the Holy Spirit when we make a public confession that Jesus Christ is our Lord and Savior. We then move from flesh to the Spirit. The Spirit of God comes to dwell inside of us. Anyone who does not have the Spirit of Christ does not belong to him *(Romans 8:9)*

The Holy Spirit baptism is a promise or guarantee of the Christian's future and eternal inheritance with Jesus Christ.

> *The Spirit himself bears witness with our spirit that we are children of God. The Holy Spirit tells us that we are not our own and that we were bought with a price.*
>
> *1 Corinthians 6:19*

The indwelt of the Holy Spirit helps protect against the enemy's attack. For if we live by the flesh, we will die, but if by the Spirit we put to death the deeds of the body, we will live. God's Spirit protects us and promises our eternity with the Lord. The work of the Holy Spirit in a believer's life is in two ways. There is first the indwelling of the Holy Spirit in a believer, and second, the filling of the Holy Spirit in a believer. Thus, all believers in Jesus Christ have God's Spirit inside them, or dwelling within them *(John 14:16, Ephesians 1:13, 2 Corinthians 1:22, and Ephesians 4:30)*, but not all believers live filled or controlled by the Holy Spirit's power. Therefore, believers have all of the Holy Spirit, but the Holy Spirit may not have all of them. You are born again when you submit to the Holy Spirit inside you after you get saved. Therefore, once saved and saved forever is a false positive.

It is not always true because you can lose your salvation if you turn your back on the Lord Jesus Christ. Each believer experiences a different filling of the Holy Spirit. On a negative note, a believer can "quench" or "grieve" the Holy Spirit *(1 Thessalonians 5:19; and Ephesians 4:30).* Almost all believers have one way or the other quench or grieve the Holy Spirit in their lifetime by sinful acts or stubbornness. On a positive note, if a believer in Christ lives in obedience to God's will, he/she should expect to see God's Spirit living through them. Being filled by the Spirit is a dynamic process of God's Spirit working in a believer's life, not a one-time event. As a believer commits his/her faith in Christ, the Holy Spirit increasingly controls or fills his/her life. This Spirit-filled life may bring about the fruits of the Spirit in a believer's life.

> *"The fruits of the Spirit in a believer's life may include love, joy, peace, patience, kindness, goodness, faithfulness, gentleness, self-control"*
>
> **Galatians 5:22**

Without the infilling of God's Spirit, people are not able to produce fruitful lives that reflect the desires of God.

5. Get Real with the Word of God

The moment you declare Jesus Christ as his/her Lord and Savior, the Holy Spirit comes in to dwell inside you. At that point, God's seal offers the promise of eternal life *(John 3:16)* because salvation is based on God's grace through faith in Jesus Christ (*(Ephesians 2:8-9).* The seal of the Holy Spirit welcomes you to the Commonwealth of God's children and protects them against forces of evil.

Once saved and saved forever is a false positive because if you go back and eat your old vomits, you will surely lose your salvation. Conservative statistics show that out of every 100 Christians who get saved, only one keeps his/her salvation forever. As we build a closer relationship with the Holy Spirit, he will pull us away sometimes from things we have in our lives that do not please Him. For instance, He will resist us from listening to inappropriate music that will hurt us spiritually because of the negative lyrics.

Allow the Holy Spirit to work in your life 24/7. The Holy Spirit will bring you the truth and will help you to cope with the fight for the truth. However, the world rejects the workings of the Holy Spirit because they can neither recognize nor understand Him as they organize their lives and leave God out of it. The Holy Spirit cannot manifest in our lives because we are too busy to wait in silence, in expectation, and in prayer for the Holy Spirit to come to us. The Holy Spirit manifested in me during my second year at the University of Ghana, Legon, during the all-night prayers by the University Christian Fellowship in 1978. One Saturday, after my one-day fasting, I decided to join my Christian brothers and sisters on Campus to worship all night. I experienced my first speaking of tongues, and my tongues were over everyone else, and I learned that it was in the Hebrew language. It just burst out my mouth, and I spoke for more than one hour according to my friends. I had read from the book of Acts, but I experienced it myself. From that very date, every time that I worship and get spiritual, my tongues will flow unconsciously. Since the day I received the Holy Spirit and began to speak in other tongues, I have never run out of inspiration. Holy Spirit is my number one driving force in my life and every true believer of Jesus Christ. Without Him, my life is dull, empty, and useless. Christianity without the operation of the Holy Spirit is mere religion. Evangelism will be difficult without the working of the Holy Spirit in our lives. We walk, sit, sleep, and do everything with the Holy Spirit. He is our soldier and 24/7 operator. We reject our Comforter, the one who makes us brave and gives us the courage to fight the good fight of faith, to take the step of faith, to do our work for Christ and His Church; Advocate (the one who will give us wisdom- a real gift which only comes from God, the one who knows the answers-our defense and expert witness), and Helper and Counselor (the one who will advise us and support us through thick and thin, the one who will fight on our behalf) because we do not have time to wait upon God, and His coming is to set our hearts on fire.

There are two most important words many people do not want to hear, and they are :(i) death and (ii) heaven. Death is when you take your last breath on earth. According to C.S Lewis, the statistics on death are impressive so far, it is one out of one and that we are faced with the reality of dying every second of every day. Death is not our final destination but a doorway to our final journey. Death is the point beyond which we do not return to life on earth. The ultimate question for Christians is, where will you be one minute after you die? Whether you believe it or not, Jesus Christ told us about two major roads the dead will pass. The narrow road that leads to heaven and the broad road (where many people pass) leads to hell.

> ***"Enter ye in at the strait gate: for wide is the gate, and broad is the way, that leadeth to destruction, and many there be which go in there at. Because strait is the gate, and narrow is the way, which leadeth unto life, and few there be that find it"***
>
> ***Matthew 7:13-14.***

The road we choose and the final destination are determined in one's lifetime. When one dies, his/her book is closed and destination determined. Which road you walk on at death depends on if you are really born again or a Nicodemus-Pharisee believer. Our admission to heaven is secured because of what Jesus Christ did on the cross. He purchased our heaven ticket for our entrance to heaven. His last words on the cross, "it is finished," stamped our heaven ticket, paid in full. All travelers desiring to enter heaven have to accept their tickets, trust in what Jesus has already done for them. Jesus Christ's death and resurrection have given the privilege, the hope, and the certainty of entering heaven. Heaven is not for one ethnic group, special denomination, certain social status, personality trait, nationality, and others. Jesus opens his arms to all and welcomes everybody to heaven if you walk on the narrow road, trusting in what He did on the cross and accepting the free gift of grace.

The new birth (BA degree) is purely the work of the Holy Spirit. It is not a stepwise process as Nicodemus might have thought. Many religious communities believe that if you are a good person and you follow all the religious protocols like Nicodemus, then you earn your ticket to heaven. It is not so but comes randomly as the wind blows.

John 3:8 gives a perfect narrative that "the wind blows wherever it pleases." You hear its sounds, but you cannot tell where it comes from or where it is going. So it is with everyone born of the Spirit". The radical change that needs to happen in your life is beyond your control. It is only God who can bring the change that needs to happen in your life to earn a heaven ticket (BA degree). There are going to be surprises now and future surprises at the heaven gate if the grace of God does not come to us through the cross and the resurrection of Jesus Christ. Many Nicodemus-like Christians who think they are heaven-bound will miss it to the advantage of thieves, armed robbers, prostitutes, alcoholics, and the like who many have labeled as hell-bound. Many who die or live without the Holy Spirit may be faced with this reality "There shall be weeping and gnashing of teeth when ye shall see Abraham, and Isaac, and Jacob, and all the prophets, in the kingdom of God, and you thrust out".

Today, many like Nicodemus do not understand what Jesus meant when he told Nicodemus that "you must be born again." It has to do with the acronym ABC. A→ Admit your sin and come to only Christ in true humility and need (Repentance), B→ Believe that Jesus is the resurrected Son of God and trust that He alone can save you from the deadly consequences of sin, and C→ Confess your faith, as the Bible tells us that if we confess with our mouth the Lord Jesus Christ and believe in our hearts that God has raised Him from the dead, we will be saved and enjoy eternal salvation. Therefore, we are called to believe and simply get saved, but salvation remains a stumbling block for everybody.

Nicodemus could not save himself, and nobody can save himself or herself. The flesh can only produce flesh. Your good works cannot earn you a BA degree (Heaven ticket). Therefore, it is the Spirit who gives birth to spirit. Again, the new birth is the work of the Holy Spirit. The Holy Spirit gives new birth, and he moves like the wind. It is by His grace that those of us who were at the back door and have now been called to share dinner/lunch with the Lord of mercy. Nobody has control over the direction of the wind and cannot predict where the wind will go. Salvation is only by the grace of God through the crucified and resurrected Jesus Christ, who is alive and sitting at the right-hand side of God today.

Everybody needs a BA degree. It does not matter whether you are a Pope, Bishop, Arch-Bishop, Prophet, Pastor, Elder, Deacon, Deaconess, and other workmen of God. You must be born again in order to enter into heaven. The anointing on you is for the service of God and does not gain you direct admission to heaven. It is by the Grace of God and by checking your spiritual barometer of exhaling the impure thoughts (confessing your sins daily) and inhaling pure thoughts (surrendering the control of your life to Christ, and appropriate the fullness of the Holy Spirit by faith).

Like Nicodemus, many Christians are caught up between carnality and spirituality (wavering in their walk with the Lord). They are not born again because they are neither cold nor hot. By my conservative estimate, about 98.0 percent of Christians vacillate between carnality and spirituality.

6. Final Thoughts.

The Holy Spirit is a divine person, and He is the third person of the trinity. Holy Spirit is God Himself and equally shares authority and power with the Father and His Son. He is dwelling in every Christian who professes publically that Jesus Christ is his/her Lord and personal savior. He does more for us including, teaching and instructing, advising, comforting, combatting, and counseling. He is an active Comforter who is comforted by deeds and a successful Comforter who never attempts what he cannot accomplish. He is also an ever-present help in time trouble. However, He does not work for every Christian, especially those who grieve or quench Him.

The Holy Spirit gives new birth, and he moves like the wind. Nobody controls what the wind does and predicts where the wind goes. Again, nobody can give himself or herself new birth, and everything you give birth to is yourself. It is only God who can bring the change that needs to happen in your life through Jesus Christ. It is indeed the Spirit that gives birth to Spirit. The new birth is purely the work of the Holy Spirit. BA (Born again) degree is issued from God and by the Holy Spirit through our Lord Jesus Christ. Nobody can save himself/herself by their personality traits-titles, accolades, social and economic positions, and actions. Your good works cannot earn eternal salvation because nobody is without sin (we have all fallen short of the grace of God). It is by the grace of God that we are counted worthy to earn eternal salvation. It is beyond our imagination how eternal life comes to us through Jesus Christ, who died on a cross, bearing the curse of our sins. Whoever looks and believes in Jesus Christ shall not perish but have eternal life. We all perish if we take our eyes off Jesus Christ; we lose our BA degree and eternal salvation.

The kingdom of God is upside-down, inverted, and bottom-up shape to religious Christians or modern-day Pharisees because Jesus Christ is a clever and revolutionary teacher who overthrows the world governing principles of our lives by means of his own death and resurrection for our sins. Consequently, those who come to Jesus Christ with childlike trust will be received and advanced in His kingdom more than those who are self-dependent and cling to earthly treasures such as money, houses, cars, accomplishments, and many more. The humble and childlike faith in Matthew 19:13-15 is contrasted to the proud, worldly, and money-loving young man because the proud and self-reliant Christians cannot enter His kingdom.

> ***"Then were there brought unto him little children that he should put his hands on them, and pray: and the disciples rebuked them. But Jesus said; suffer little children, and forbid them not to come unto me: for of such is the***

kingdom of heaven. And he laid his hands on them and departed thence"

(Matthew 19: 13).

Most of today's Christians are like Nicodemus because he privately went in the night to see Jesus, and many struggled with the public profession of their faith in Jesus. They go to church, hold high positions such as pastors, prophets, elders, and more, but they are full of themselves (not Christ-centered). Nicodemus was shocked and did not want to hear from Jesus Christ that he was not heaven material. Today many Christians do not want the truth because they cannot handle it. Like Nicodemus, your good work is not good enough before the Lord Jesus. We all need to be born again in water and spirit, but we fall short of heaven's mark. We need a total makeover by Jesus Christ. We need to take a hard look at Jesus Christ on the cross and get convicted. Take a second, look at Jesus' resurrection, and get converted. Your whole life must be remade and relived to earn a born-again degree and paid-in-full heaven ticket.

The parallel of Numbers 21:8 and John 3:14-15 in explaining the born again question. Just as Moses lifted up the snake in the desert, so the Son of Man must be lifted up, that everyone who believes in Him may have eternal life. Looking at the snake on the pole is a picture of what it means to believe in Jesus Christ and his death for us on the cross. There is a price to get saved in the Moses era and the same with before and after Jesus. Salvation in Moses' era involved a snake bite, and pre and post-Jesus involves radical transformation and humble repentance. The final stage of salvation is at looking to the snake or Jesus and getting saved forever. Salvation starts with God and ends with His Son Jesus Christ. God so loved the world that He gave his one and only Son that whosoever believes in Him shall not perish but have eternal life *(John3:16).* Real born again means looking at the great drops of blood (sweats) of Jesus at Gethsemane, Jesus hanging on the cross, dying on the cross and buried thereafter, rising up, ascending to heaven, and sitting at the Father's right hand.

The road from carnality to spirituality is very slippery, and very few reach there.

7. Concluding Remarks:

To be born again is to be saved eternally. BA degree candidates experience a spiritual transformation. Today, many Christians like Nicodemus struggle to understand the meaning of "Born again." Jesus is still telling us that no one enters the kingdom of God without a BA degree. Nobody can save himself or herself by good works because flesh can only give birth to flesh, but Spirit gives birth to spirit. Everybody needs a change of heart which is the work of the Holy Spirit by God, the death of Christ on the cross (cleansing away our past, present, and future sins), and the resurrection of Jesus Christ (Jesus is still alive and lives forever). Therefore, to be born again is to die in flesh with Jesus Christ at Calvary, resurrect with Jesus Christ, and live with Jesus Christ forever *(1 Corinthians 15: 1-4).* Shamefully burying our old lives, we experience a spiritual rebirth. To be born again is to have a relationship with God, receive spiritual life through Jesus Christ, and enjoy the fruits of the Spirit.

The ABC of receiving salvation (BA degree) is as follows: A→ Admit your sins and come to Jesus Christ in true humility and need. You repent and turn around to go in a new direction, B→ Believe that Jesus is the resurrected Son of God and trust that He alone can save you from the deadly consequences of sin. Believe that Jesus not only shed His blood and died for us, but that He rose from the dead and is still alive and active today, and C→ Confess your faith, as Scripture tells us if we confess with our mouth the Lord Jesus and believe in our heart that God has raised Him from the dead, we will be saved. Just Believe in the Lord Jesus with all your heart, soul, and mind, and you will be saved. We embrace Jesus as our Lord and Savior and imitate His life. When we become born again, we recognize God as our father and become His children. You must allow Christ to take your life in a new direction.

The Christian life can fall into three categories: (1) the natural man (one who has not received Christ as personal Lord and Savior), lives a self-centered life, and Christ is outside his life. He is in charge, and his interests are directed by himself, resulting in discord and frustration.

> ***"But the natural man receiveth not the things of the Spirit of God: for they are foolishness unto him: neither can he know them, because they are spiritually discerned"***

1 Corinthians 2:14

(2) Spiritual man (one who is directed and empowered by the Holy Spirit), L leads Christ-directed life. Christ is on the throne, and self is yielding to Christ. He who is spiritual appraises all things and has the mind of Christ.

"But he that is spiritual judgeth all things, yet he himself is he himself is judged of no man" 1 Corinthians 2:15

and (3) the carnal man (One who has received Christ, but who lives in defeat because he is trying to live the Christian life in his own strength). He leads a self-directed life, and self is on the throne. Christ is dethroned and not allowed to direct his life.

> ***"And I, brethren, could not speak unto you as unto spiritual, but as unto carnal, even as unto babes in Christ. I have fed you with milk, and not with meat: for hitherto ye were not able to bear it, neither yet now are ye able. For ye are yet carnal: for whereas there is among you envying, and strife, and divisions, are ye carnal and walk as men?'***

1 Corinthians 3: 1-3

Why are few Christians experiencing abundant and fruitful life? Many Christians are carnal because they go to church, but Jesus Christ is not their Lord and personal savior. Most Christians waver or vacillate between carnality and spirituality. Spiritual Christians (few) are real born again individuals with the following personality traits: Christ-centered, trust God, obey God, empowered by Holy Spirit, witness Christ to others who profess to be effective prayer warriors, understand God's word, and full of love, joy, peace, patience, kindness, faithfulness, and goodness. Carnal Christians (many) struggle with born again questions and have the following personality traits: self-centered, ignorance of spiritual heritage, discouragement, disobedience, unbelief, guilt, worry, jealousy, critical spirit, no desire for Bible study, loss of love for God and others, legalistic attitude, impure thoughts, poor prayer life, frustration, and aimlessness. Thus, carnal individuals who profess to be Christians can continue to the fullness of the Holy Spirit (*Ephesians 5:5*). Walking in the Spirit means a Christian can live in Spirit-directed lifestyles: Your life will demonstrate more and more of the fruits of the Spirit and will be more and more conformed to the image of Christ, your prayer life and Bible studies will become meaningful, you will experience His power in witnessing *(Acts 1:8)*, you will be prepared for spiritual conflict against the world, against the flesh, and against Satan, and you will experience His power to resist temptation and sin. To maintain spiritual equilibrium (keep your heaven ticket), you need spiritual breathing of exhaling the impure and inhaling the pure. It is an exercise in faith that enables you to continue to experience God's love and forgiveness.

Exhaling involves confessing your sins, agreeing with God concerning your sin, and thanking Him for His forgiveness of it, according to *1 John 1:9 and Hebrews 10: 1-25*. Confession is all about repentance (a change in attitude and action). Inhaling involves surrendering the control of your life to Christ, and appropriately receiving the fullness of the Holy Spirit by faith, trusting that He now directs and empowers you according to the Scriptures. **Ephesians 5:18, and the** promise of *1 John 5:14-15.* However, many Christians may receive the Holy Spirit and lose it because there is no continuous spiritual breathing.

8. *Let's Pray*

Father help me [*Insert your name about here*] to admit that nothing good dwells in me. Jesus, impart your own life into me and let me live as a new baby in your arms. The peace of God that passes all our understanding keeps my heart and mind center in Christ Jesus until life everlasting. Father, thank you for sending your Holy Spirit to me [*insert your name about here*] in Jesus' name. God, I know that I have sinned against you and am deserving of punishment. But Jesus Christ took the punishment that I deserve so that through faith in Him, I could be forgiven. I place my trust in Him alone for salvation. Thank you for your wonderful grace and forgiveness—the gift of eternal life. Whatever it takes, Lord, fill me [*insert your name about here*] with the Holy Spirit and any gifting you would be pleased to give me.

I [*insert your name about here*] open my heart to Christ. I want him to take over my life. I want to be sure that I am on the narrow road. I want to change my way of living. I confess that I have sinned. I want Jesus as my Savior and Lord and Master, and I want to be sure of it. Lord Jesus, I want to know you personally. Thank you for dying on the cross for my sins.

I open the door of my life to you and ask you to come in as my Savior and Lord. Take control of my life. Thank you for forgiving my sins (past, today, and future) and giving me eternal life. Make me the kind of person you want me to be.

Dear Father, I need You. I acknowledge that I have been directing my own life and that, as a result, I have sinned against You. I thank You that You have forgiven my sins through Christ's death on the cross for me. I now invite Christ to again take His place on the throne of my life. Fill me with the Holy Spirit as You commanded me to be filled, and as You promised in Your Word that You would do if I asked in faith. I now thank You for directing my life and for filling me with the Holy Spirit. O Lord, who has mercy upon all, takes away from me my sins, and mercifully kindles in me the fire of your Holy Spirit. Take away from me the heart of stone, and give me a heart of flesh, a heart to love and adore You, a heart to delight in You, to follow and enjoy You, for Christ's sake. I will use the Sword of the Spirit by speaking the Word of God as it applies to whatever situation I may face today. Father, please remind me of your Word via the Holy Spirit. I will continue to pray in the Spirit throughout the day and intercede for all Christians as the Holy Spirit prompts me. I believe that the Holy Spirit is interceding on my behalf according to my prayers.

O Lord, fill me afresh with the power of your spirit in Jesus' name. O Lord, heal every wounded part of my life through the power of the Holy Spirit. O Lord, by the help of your spirit, let my life reflect the life of God in Jesus' name. Sweet Holy Spirit, I want to be connected to you forever in Jesus' name. Dear Holy Spirit, enrich me with Your gifts in Jesus' name. Dear Holy Spirit, quicken me and increase my desire for the things of heaven. Dear Holy Spirit, lay Your hands upon me and quench every rebellion in me in Jesus' name. Holy Ghost fire, begin to burn away every self-centeredness in me, in the name of Jesus. Holy Spirit let your power flow like blood into my veins. Dear Holy Spirit, continue to show forth your manifest presence in my life in Jesus' name. Let my feet become the thunder of God as I stamp them. Let them deafen the enemy in the name of Jesus. Holy Spirit, let all my divinely-appointed helpers begin to locate me from now, in the name of Jesus. Dear Holy Spirit, thank you for causing me to ride above principalities and powers in the name of Jesus. Father, thank you for the empowerment of the Holy Spirit. Amen.

Let the eyes of our understanding be enlightened that we might know the hope of our calling, the riches of the glory of our inheritance in the saints, and exceeding greatness of your power toward us, who believe *(Ephesians 1:17-18)*. Strengthen us with might by your Spirit in the inner man *(Ephesians 3:16)*. Father God, I *[insert your name about here]* know that I have broken your laws, and my sins have separated me from you. I am very sorry, and now I want to turn away from my past sinful life toward you. Please forgive me, and help me avoid sinning again. I believe that your son, Jesus Christ died for my sins, was resurrected from the dead, is alive, and hears my prayer. I *[insert your name about here]* invite Jesus to become the Lord of my life, to rule and reign in my heart from this day forward. Please send your Holy

Spirit to help me obey You and to do Your will for the rest of my life. In Jesus' name, I pray, Amen.

Every evil door that is giving my enemies way in my life be closed now by the blood of Jesus in the name of Jesus. I *[insert your name about here]* use the blood of Jesus to lose myself from every spirit in me which is not a Spirit of God in the name of Jesus. Let the divine anointing for spiritual breakthrough fall upon me now, in the name of Jesus. I shall not die, but live, and declare the works of the Lord **(Psalm 118:17).** I *[insert your name about here]* receive power to operate with sharp spiritual eyes that cannot be deceived in the name of Jesus. Let the glory and power of the Almighty God fall upon my life in a mighty way, in the name of Jesus.

Jesus Christ defeated the whole kingdom of darkness and won an overwhelming victory by disarming principalities and powers at the cross. Jesus is the victor. He is a mighty conqueror. Jesus triumphed over all his foes, and he has given me complete victory over every foe in my life. This includes a victory over Satan, demons, and the whole kingdom of darkness, as well as victory over all works of darkness, including witches and wizards. Therefore, Satan, demons, witches, and warlocks, you have absolutely no power and no authority over me. Lord Jesus, let your kingdom come in the power of the Holy Spirit and glory of God. I *[insert your name about here]* seal this prayer with the precious blood of the Great Shepherd of the sheep and with thanksgiving. Amen.

Chapter 5
Trading Heaven for Hell

"Are you so foolish? Having begun in the spirit, are you now being made perfect by flesh? Have you suffered so many things in vain? If indeed, it was in vain"

Galatians 3:3-4

"For the love of money is a root of all kinds of evil, for which some have strayed from the faith in their greediness and pierced themselves through with many sorrows"

1 Timothy 6:10

"Beloved, I beg you as sojourners and pilgrims, abstain from fleshly lusts which war against the soul"

1 Peter 2:11

"For you shall worship no other god, for the Lord, whose name is Jealous, is a jealous God"

Exodus 34:14

"My sons, if sinners entice you, do not consent."

Proverbs 1:10

"Behold these are the ungodly who prosper in the world, they increase in riches"

Psalm 73:12

1. Introduction

The Christian race is a daily commitment with the Lord. We do not rest on our oars because we stand to lose our salvation as quickly as we receive it. Lot's wife lost her salvation momentarily by looking back at Sodom and Gomorrah. She could not get Sodom and Gomorrah off her mind and slipped to the devil's side. Millions of Christians are trading Heaven for Hell by getting hooked to all the lust, flesh, and pride of this world, which are passing away quickly.

"So it came to pass when they had brought them outside that he said, escape for your life. Do not look behind you nor stay anywhere in the plain. Escape to the mountains, lest you be destroyed. But his wife looked back behind him, and she became a pillar of salt"

Genesis 19:17&26

Saul, the first anointed king of Israel, traded heaven for hell because he disobeyed God for his fear of men. Many believers stand to lose their salvation because they fear men more than

God. Why? We see people with our eyes but we feel the presence of God in the spirit.

> ***"So Samuel said; Has the Lord as great delight in burnt offerings and sacrifices? As in obeying the voice of the Lord? Behold, to obey is better than sacrifice. And to heed than the fat of rams. For rebellion is the sin of witchcraft. And stubbornness is as iniquity and idolatry. Because you have rejected the word of the Lord, he also has rejected you from being king. Then Saul said to Samuel, I have sinned, for I have transgressed the commandment of the Lord and your words because I feared the people and obeyed their voice"***

> ***1 Samuel 15:22-24***

Saul's heart was not after God but men. He was a man-pleaser, and many of us are king Saul's incarnates. However, David did more evil than Saul, but God accepted him because his heart was after God. God judges us by the content of our hearts. Our hearts should always be after God even when we sin. In order not to lose our salvation, prophet Jeremiah inspires us here.

> ***"Whether it is pleasing or displeasing, we will obey the voice of the Lord, our God to whom we send you that it may be well with us when we obey the voice of the Lord our God"***

> ***Jeremiah 42:6***

Dear Christians, we should put on childlike confidence in God and seek His divine guidance so that we can stand the storms in our lives. When you run into life-threatening situations, many will advise you on what to do, but listen to what God tells you. Listen to the person of the Holy Spirit who is gently talking to you.

Many believers and unbelievers are ready to exchange heaven for money (Mammon) and, the attendant evils. God is not worried about His children having riches but worried about riches having His children. We are not condemning riches because many of God's friends, such as Abraham, Jacob, Joseph, and David (to mention but a few), were rich in their days. It is what happens to our hearts when we become rich. If we focus on money and put God behind us, we fall into its snare and temptations. The greed and the pride make believers puff up and disregard the commandments of God.

> *"But those who desire to be rich fall into temptation and a snare, and into many foolish and harmful lusts which drown men in destruction and perdition (eternal damnation, or hell). But you, O man of God (believer), flee these things and pursue righteousness, godliness, faith, love, patience, gentleness"*
>
> *1 Timothy 6:9&11*

It does not add up by spending a few years in happiness on earth and the rest of your life in eternal hell. Many believers and workmen of God are in the ministry of Christ today because of prosperity (getting something from God) but not what God can get out of them (divine relationship with God). Most people spend their lives in wealth and riches and in a moment, go down to the grave. We are aware of the bible story of the death of two men, the poor man (Lazarus) and the rich man. The rich man was happy for the number of years he spent on the earth (maybe 70years, 100years, or 120years, etc.), but the poor man was tormented in all the days of his life on earth. After their death, the poor man was found in the bosom of Abraham (heaven), and the rich man was in hades for eternity. Many smart people are short-changing their lives (spending a few years in happiness on earth) for staying in hell forever. Matthew has warned us about the pitfall of earthly glory.

> ***"For what profit is it to a man if he gains the whole world and loses his own soul? Or what will a man give in exchange for his soul?"***
>
> ***Matthew 16:26***

Why should we cheat, kill and even destroy to gain riches and wealth for a moment and quickly fall into hell forever? Instant gratification (quick pleasures of life), such as money, drugs, sex, and the rest is taking millions to hell. There is hope in waiting on God. There are times when waiting appears like just losing time, but it is not so. The enemy will always try to discourage us but wait on God because true riches come from Him.

As I write this chapter, I am wondering how many believers and unbelievers are being deceived by men and women to engage in improper sexual practices that can lead to their ultimate spiritual and physical deaths. Sex, the oldest and effective trick of the devil that has taken millions to hell, is the least talked about topic in the ministry of Christ. Many pastors, saints, and other workmen of God feel very uneasy at the mention of sex, but these people have fallen victims to it. Why has the enemy used sex as bait to woo many to hell? Most people live in the flesh, and the flesh is weaker than the spirit, so many fall into the snare of sex. Sexual lusts almost destroyed the saints of God: the relationship between Samson and Delilah, David and Bathsheba, and Solomon and Sheba, only to mention but a few. Paul has warned us to be strong in the spirit and the power of His might because in our flesh the enemy will always defeat us. We cannot deal with sexual perversion without staying strong in the spirit and binding the demons concerned with the blood of Jesus.

"Do you not know that the unrighteous will not inherit the kingdom of God? Do not be deceived. Neither fornicators (those who date and engage in physical sex before marriage), nor idolaters, nor adulterers coveting one's wife or husband and engaging in physical sex), nor homosexuals, nor sodomites, nor thieves, nor covetous, nor drunkards, nor revilers, nor extortioners will inherit the kingdom of God. Or do you know that your body is the temple of the Holy Spirit who is in you, who you have from God, and you are not your own"

1 Corinthians 6:9-10&19

Note that anxiety produces depression, and depression creates emptiness. Many people try to fill up their emptiness with lustful sins, such as alcohol, drugs, sex, and many more but to no avail. If you are overburdened with fear, which is the heart of anxiety, I would encourage you to strengthen yourself each day with the 365 "fear nots" in the bible. There is a true story told by a friend of mine on a well-known lustful sin of our time (sex). Jane (not her real name) is a married woman who went to a small grocery store. She met Valentine (not his real name), a married man in the store. Valentine cast lustful sight on Jane and asked for her home phone number. Jane politely gave her the phone number but added that the number belonged to the husband. Valentine refused to take the phone number because he wanted to speak to Jane and not her husband. Valentine had the wrong mindset, and if Jane had not known Jesus, the two would have committed adultery in the process of getting to know each other on the phone. Many are losing their salvation at the margins. Thus, a life is lost forever in five or minutes in an illegal sexual relationship. Many are willing to trade their lives (maybe 30years, 40years, 50years, etc.) for five or ten-minute sexual gratification. The journey of sexual fantasy in which lives are lost forever is not smart but many are running into such fantasies in great numbers.

> ***"Flee sexual immorality. Every sin that a man does is outside the body, but he who commits sexual immorality sins against his own body"***
>
> ***1 Corinthians 6:18***

Satan has set several traps in the form of sex, drugs, alcohol, money, fashion, idols, pride, and varying kinds to make you trade in heaven for hell.

> ***"In latter days, many believers will walk away from faith because of offence, lack of patience in waiting on God, worldly pleasures, and varying ungodly practices. Now, the Spirit expressly says that in the latter times, some will depart the faith giving heed to deceiving spirits and doctrines of demons"***

> ***1 Timothy 4:1***

Most people turn from the faith because they see evildoers prospering in their ways. When we see men around us prosper and be happy, while they forsake God's ways and we are left in difficulty or suffering, we are in danger of first fretting at what appears so strange and then gradually yielding to seek our prosperity in their paths.

> ***"I have seen the wicked in great power and spreading himself like a native green tree. Yet he passed away, and behold, he was no more, indeed, I sought him, but he could not be found"***

> ***Psalm 37:35-36***

Let us not focus on the worldly gains of unbelievers but on God. God works continually in us, but sometimes we are blinded by unbelief. Do not limit God's thoughts in your life because He is bigger than what you can imagine. When you are in the valley or difficult spots, you must work continually in obedience to the word of God to complete His plan in you.

> ***"The Lord upholds all who fall and rises up all who are bowed down. The eyes of all look expectantly to you, and you give them their food in due season"***
>
> ***Psalm 145:14-15***

If we focus on the wealth and riches of the ungodly men, we are likely to trade heaven for hell. We should not become Christians in Galatia who started well in spirit, but finished in flesh.

> ***"So the last will be first, and the first last. For many are called, but few chosen"***
>
> ***Matthew 20:16***

Brothers and sisters in Christ, we are stepping into perilous times, and Paul has warned us in his second letter to Timothy.

> ***"For men will be lovers of themselves, lovers of money, boasters, proud, blasphemers, disobedient to parents, unthankful, unholy, unloving, unforgiving, slanders, without self-control, brutal, despisers of good"***
>
> ***2 Timothy 3:2-3***

Yes, and all who desire to live godly in Christ Jesus will suffer persecution, but do not trade in heaven for hell. Hang onto the Cross of Jesus, and you will surely wear the crown of gold in His second coming.

2. *Are you Thinking of the City of God or City of man?*

In his classic book, *The City of God*, St. Augustine promoted a non-futurist view of the Millennium -- that the era the Bible refers to as the Millennium is actually the present, ongoing rule of Christ in the church with the saints. This view prevailed through most of the Middle Ages and through the Reformation. Some call this view "amillennialism."

In Christian eschatology, it involves the rejection of the belief that Jesus will have a literal, thousand-year-long, physical reign on the earth.

There are many theologians in recent years who have once again adopted St. Augustine's position. Among them is Dr. J. Rodman Williams of Regent University. In his book, *Renewal Theology*, he writes, "I prefer to speak of a present and historical millennium on earth and not in heaven. To be sure, it is a heavenly existence while yet on this earth, for truly we are blessed "in Christ with every spiritual blessing in the heavenly places" **(Ephesians. 1:3).** Even now we "reign in life through the one man Jesus Christ" **(Romans. 5:17).** Throughout the whole Christian era, whatever their lot, the saints live and reign "with Christ a thousand years." A present millennium is totally other than "no millennium": it is the reality of the present kingdom of God."

Regardless of when the thousand-year rule of Christ occurs, we can rejoice that He is coming soon and declare with all the saints, **"Maranatha** -- even so, come Lord Jesus."

In sharp contrast are those who live and think of the City of Man (our present world). We are living in a society of instant gratification, material comfort, and endless indulgences. And the church has become worldly. Nothing demonstrates that I don't think any more graphically than the lack of interest in heaven. Most Christians are, to some degree or another, more interested in laying up treasure on earth than in heaven. They are more concerned with their investments, their retirement package, and their own future on earth than they are with heaven. I suppose most Christians sacrifice the eternal blessing of glory on the altar of temporal gratification. We do not talk about heaven much. We do not sing about heaven much because we are really not that interested.

The old song said "heaven on my mind," but that is not really true anymore. Because believers do not have heaven on their minds, waste their lives, hinder the power of the church, and they are consumed with fading things.

I think, throughout the history of the church, heaven has been a preoccupation of God's people. Many songs have focused on heaven. Because people through the years in the life of the church, have been loosely tied to earth, and so they have longed for heaven. I suppose even this time in the history of the world around the globe, where Christians don't have it as comfortably as we do; there is still great anticipation for heaven.

Most Christians, I suppose, through the centuries could say with the psalmist in Psalm 73:25, "Whom have I in heaven but Thee and besides Thee I desire nothing on earth." That is the expression of the heart that longs for God. Much like Psalm 42:1, where the psalmist says, "As the deer pants after the water brook, so pants my soul after Thee, O God." The psalmist in the same Psalm 73:26 said, "Nearness to God is my good." He said, "God is my portion forever." Being preoccupied with the person of God, longing to be in the presence of God was on the heart of Christians.

In fact, the pure in heart, according to the words of Jesus in the Beatitudes, are promised that they will one day see God. Through the centuries that desire to see God, to be in God's presence, to enjoy God forever, that desire that there is nothing in the world that can satisfy man has been on the hearts of believers. But it is not so in this culture where people trust in the city of man more than the city of God — the new Jerusalem.

The presence of God assures an entirely new state for those who inhabit the new Jerusalem. In contrast to their former suffering, which included going through the tribulation for many of these saints, God is stated to "wipe away all tears from their eyes." There is no just ground for imagining from this chapter that the saints will shed tears in heaven concerning the failures of their former life on earth. The emphasis here is on the comfort of God, not on the remorse of the saints. The tears seem to refer to tears shed on earth as the saints' endured suffering for Christ's sake, rather than tears shed in heaven because of human failure. This is in keeping with the rest of the passage, which goes on to say that other aspects of human sorrow such as death, sorrow, crying, or pain will also be no more in existence. The summary given at the end of the verse is "The former things are passed away." The "crying" mentioned refers to the vocal response to sorrow in contrast to tears which are a silent response. The new situation is the consummation of divine grace and the assurance of the estate of ineffable blessedness for those who were once lost sinners. The Scriptures make plain that not only the old earth and heaven pass away but also all the details and associations that belong to it which would mar the situation in the new heaven and the new earth.

3. *Get Real with the Word*

It does not add up by spending a few years in happiness on earth and the rest of your life in eternal hell. Many believers and workmen of God are in the ministry of Christ today because of prosperity (getting something from God) but not what God can get out of them (divine relationship with God). Most people spend their lives in wealth and riches, and a moment goes down to the grave. We are aware of the bible story of the death of two men, the poor man (Lazarus) and the rich man. The rich man was happy for the number of years he spent on the earth (maybe 70years, 100years, or 120years, etc.), but the poor man was tormented in all the days of his life on earth. After their death, the poor man was found in the bosom of Abraham (heaven), and the rich man was in hades. Many smart people are short-changing their lives (spending a few years in happiness on earth) for staying in hell forever. Matthew has warned us about the pitfall of earthly glory.

Why should we cheat, kill and even destroy to gain riches and wealth for a moment and quickly fall into hell forever? Instant gratification (quick pleasures of life), such as money, drugs, sex, and the rest is taking millions to hell. There is hope in waiting on God. There are times when waiting appears like just losing time, but it is not so. The enemy will always try to discourage us but wait on God because true riches come from Him.

The Lord is constantly telling us not to fear because He is with us to help us deal victoriously with the realities of life.

"Teaching them to observe all things whatsoever I have commanded you: and, lo, I am with you always, even unto the end of the world. Amen"

Matthew 28:20

When the time came for the Lord to depart physically from this world, he sent the Holy Spirit to be in and with us.

"And I will pray the Father, and he shall give you another Comforter, that he may abide with you forever. Even the Spirit of Truth, whom the World cannot receive, because it seeth him not, neither knoweth him: but ye know him; for he dwelleth with you, and shall be in you. I will not leave you comfortless: I will come to you"

John 14:16-18

The Holy Spirit comes to take place of the resurrected Christ, and He lives in you, so take advantage of His grace and power in your life. Because He is in you, you can do all things through Christ who is in you via the power of the Holy Spirit. You live in the city of God spiritually. It is impossible to live a spiritual Christian life without the person of the Holy Spirit. He is your lifeguard, teacher, instructor, and comforter. The thought of rapture is the city of God mentality. At the rapture of the church, in the twinkling of an eye, the dead in Christ shall rise first, then we who are alive and remain shall be caught up with them to meet the Lord in the air *(1 Thessalonians 4: 16-17).*

With the world spinning out of control, the will of God is revealed in *2 Peter 3:9.*

> *"The Lord is not slack concerning his promise,*
> *as some men count slackness; but longsuffering*
> *to us-ward, not willing that any should perish,*
> *but that all should come to repentance"*

The first man is of the earth, earthy (City of Man), and the second man is the Lord from heaven (the city of God) *(1 Corinthians 15:47).* We are separated from God into a life of darkness and spiritual blindness (City of Man).

Don't let Satan deceive us of who we are. We are not of this world but peculiar people from the heavenly kingdom. Though we live on earth, our citizenship is of heaven, so we operate in the kingdom of God mindset. It is a royal and glorious kingdom of priests. You were born into this kingdom the moment you became born again.

> *"Giving thanks unto our Father, which hath made us, meet to be partakers of the inheritance of the saints in light. Who hath delivered us from the power of darkness; and hath translated us into the kingdom of his dear Son"*

> *Colossians 1:12-13*

You belong to where all things are possible and operate by the law of the Spirit of life. In this kingdom, everyone is blessed, and everything you do prospers under your watch. Our joy never ends, and we also rejoice in adversities. Hallelujah! Moreover, in this eternal kingdom, we do not allow the things which are seen to determine and control the quality of our lives. We see and live by faith. We are confident that whatever we see that we do not like is subject to change.

> *"For our light affliction, which is but for a moment, worketh for us a far more exceeding and eternal weight of glory. While we look not at the things which are seen, but at the things which are not seen: for the things that are seen are temporal; but the things which are not seen are eternal"*

> *2 Corinthians 4:17-18*

This is the life of the City of God. We can do all things through Christ who strengthens us. We are forever victorious. Glory to God. Our journey in life is upward and forward to please the Lord in all things.

4. *Final Thoughts*

One of our final thoughts in this chapter is captured in the first letter of Apostle Peter:

> ***"But ye are a chosen generation, a royal priesthood, a holy nation, a peculiar people; that ye should show forth the praises of him who hath called you out of darkness into his marvelous light. Which in the time past were not a people, but are now the people of God: which had not obtained mercy, but now have obtained mercy"***

> ***1 Peter 2:9-10***

If we have been delivered from darkness unto light, we have to think and act heavenly 24/7 as St. Augustine did in his era.

Most Christians agree and think certain basic tenets regarding the last days:

- **Jesus Christ will return.**
  "And after He had said these things, He was lifted up while they were looking on, and a cloud received Him out of their sight. And as they were gazing intently into the sky while He was going, behold, two men in white clothing stood beside them. They also said, 'Men of Galilee, why do you stand looking into the sky? This Jesus, who has been taken up from you into heaven,

will come in just the same way as you have watched Him go into heaven'" (**Acts 1:9-11**).

- **Upon His return, Jesus will judge the living and the dead.**
"Then I saw a great white throne and Him who sat upon it, from whose presence earth and heaven fled away, and no place was found for them. And I saw the dead, the great and the small, standing before the throne, and books were opened; and another book was opened, which is the book of life; and the dead were judged from the things which were written in the books, according to their deeds"

Revelation 20:11-12.

- **There will be a new heaven and a new earth after Christ's return.**
"Then I saw a new heaven and a new earth; for the first heaven and the first earth passed away, and there is no longer any sea. And I saw the holy city, new Jerusalem, coming down out of heaven from God, made ready as a bride adorned for her husband. And I heard a loud voice from the throne, saying, "Behold, the tabernacle of God is among men, and He will dwell among them, and they shall be His people, and God Himself will be among them"

Revelation 21:1-3

- **There will be a resurrection for those who have died in Christ.**

  "For if we believe that Jesus died and rose again, even so, God will bring with Him those who have fallen asleep in Jesus. For this, we say to you, by the word of the Lord, that we, who are alive and remain until the coming of the Lord, will not precede those who have fallen asleep. For the Lord, Himself will descend from heaven with a shout, with the voice of the archangel and with the trumpet of God, and the dead in Christ will rise first. Then we who are alive and remain will be caught up together with them in the clouds to meet the Lord in the air, and so we shall always be with the Lord

  1 Thessalonians 4:14-17

Between the return of Christ (**Revelation 19:11-21**) and the Final Judgment (**Revelation 20:11-15**), the Apostle John gives us the description of the thousand years reign of Christ.

- Satan is bound for a thousand years: "Then I saw an angel coming down from heaven, holding the key of the abyss and a great chain in his hand. And he laid hold of the dragon, the serpent of old, who is the devil and Satan, and bound him for a thousand years; and he threw him into the abyss, and shut it and sealed it over him so that he would not deceive the nations any longer until the thousand years were completed; after these things, he must be released for a short time" **(Revelation 20:1-3).**

- Jesus Christ reigns on the earth during this time: "Then I saw thrones, and they sat on them, and judgment was given to them and I saw the souls of those who had been beheaded because of their testimony of Jesus and because of the word of God, and those who had not worshiped the beast or his image, and had not received the mark on their forehead and on their hand; and they came to life and reigned with Christ for a thousand years. The rest of the dead did not come to life until the thousand years were completed. This is the first resurrection. Blessed and holy is the one who has a part in the first resurrection; over these the second death has no power, but they will be priests of God and of Christ and will reign with Him for a thousand years" ***(Revelation 20:4-6).***

- Then after a thousand years, the final battle is fought:

"When the thousand years are completed, Satan will be released from his prison, and will come out to deceive the nations which are in the four corners of the earth, Gog and Magog, to gather them together for the war; the number of them is like the sand of the seashore. And they came upon the broad plain of the earth and surrounded the camp of the saints and the beloved city, and fire came down from heaven and devoured them. And the devil who deceived them was thrown into the lake of fire and brimstone, where the beast and the false prophet are also; and they will be tormented day and night forever and ever" ***(Revelation 20:7-10).***

5. *Let's Pray*

Father, thank you for the great hope of thinking heaven all the time. Thank you for the heavenly promises you have laid before me *(insert your name about here)*. Oh, Father, how awesome it all is. Lord, I do pray that you would cause me to set my affections on things above and not on things on the earth. Sap so much strength, so much energy, and so many resources fussing about the trivialities of this life, instead of investing our energies and our thoughts in that which is eternal. Thank You for the hope of heaven, which enables me to endure anything here in the light of what is to come. Thank You for the hope of heaven, which is the greatest incentive to excellence in my Christian character, which is the truest path to joy, which is the best defense against sin. Thank You for the hope of heaven, which strengthens my spiritual service and causes me to honor you. Help me to live in the light of the glory to come and to treat very lightly this world, for there is a far more eternal weight of glory. May I (***insert your name about here)*** hold lightly to the passing things and feel the true weight of what is eternal.

And should there be anyone in my midst, Lord, anyone who hears this message that is not on the way to heaven, I ***insert your name about here*** pray that you would save them by Your grace and turn destruction to a path to glory for Jesus' sake. Righteous Father, what a blessing it is to live in the city of God mentally. I ***insert your name about here*** walk in the light and Blessing of your indwelling presence, knowing that I am mightily helped and energized for success.

Jesus Christ defeated the whole kingdom of darkness and won an overwhelming victory by disarming principalities and powers at the cross. Jesus Christ is the victor. He is the mighty conqueror. Jesus triumphed over all his foes, and he has given me complete victory over every foe in my life. This includes a victory over Satan, the demons, and the whole kingdom of darkness, as well as victory over all works of darkness, including witches, and wizards. Therefore, Satan, demons, witches, and warlocks, you have absolutely no power and no authority over me *(Luke 10:19)*. Lord of glory; let your kingdom come through the power of the Holy Spirit and the glory of God. I *[insert your name about here]* seal this prayer with the precious blood of the Great Shepherd of the sheep and thanksgiving, In Jesus name I pray, Amen,

Chapter 6
Positive Tongue saves

Let the words of my mouth, and the meditation of my heart, be acceptable in thy sight, O Lord, my strength, and my redeemer"

Psalm 19:14

"He that keepeth his mouth keepeth his life: but he that openeth wide his lips shall have destruction"

Proverbs 13:3

"Whoso keepeth his mouth and his tongue keepeth his soul from trouble"

Proverbs 21:23

"Death and life are in the power of the tongue: and they that love it shall eat the fruit thereof"

Proverbs 18:21

"Be not rash with thy mouth, and let not thine heart be hasty to utter anything before God,

*for God is in heaven, and thou upon earth:
therefore, let thy words be few"*

Ecclesiastes 5:2

*"For by thy words thou shalt be justified, and
by thy words thou shalt be condemned"*

Matthew 12:37

*"And the tongue is a fire, a world of iniquity:
so is the tongue among our members, that it
defileth the whole body, and setteth on fire the
course of nature; and it is set on fire of hell"*

James 3:6

1. Introduction

Generally, communication with each other can either make
or unmake a relationship. What you say and how it is said
can make a whole lot of difference. Christians, in particular,
struggle in their daily conversations. Even though we know
that Scriptures have much to tell us about how we are —and
are not to use our words, this is still an immense problem,
causing headaches and strain, not only in family relationships,
but also in friendships, work, and church settings. The biblical
patriarchs such as Sarai, Moses, Naomi, David, and Peter
doubted for a while and spoke negative words.

Sarah misspoke when she doubted the Lord on the prophecy
of bearing her own son Isaac at old age.

"Is anything too hard for the Lord? At the time appointed, I will return unto thee, according to the time of life, and Sarah shall have a son. Then Sarah denied, saying, I laughed not, for she was afraid. And he said, Nay, but thou didst laugh"

Genesis 18:14-15

Today, believers like Sarah continue to doubt God's plan and speak negative words that put us in the devil's bondage for some time or forever.

Naomi, the mother-in-law of Ruth, spoke bitterly about herself and thought God had afflicted her with curses.

"And she said unto them, call me not Naomi, call me Mara; for the Almighty hath dealt very bitterly with me. I went out full, and the Lord hath brought me home again empty: why then call ye me Naomi, seeing the Lord hath testified against me, and the Almighty hath afflicted me?"

Ruth 1:-21

In the beginning, Naomi did not understand God's plan in her life because God's thoughts are not our thoughts, neither are our ways His ways because He knows the end from the beginning *(Isaiah 55:8) and (Isaiah 46:10).* In the end, God put a smile on Naomi's face by making her the grandmother of Obed, and great grandmother of Jesse, David Jesus, and all of Christians. The lesson from Naomi's story is that when you go through bitter life experiences, do not blame God and speak negative words. The bigger your troubles, the larger God's plan and Glory in your life. In every difficult corner, the enemy put you keep your mouth shut, and wait on God's deliverance. Not only did Peter deny Jesus at Gethsemane, but he cursed and swore negative words.

> **"And after a while came unto him they that stood by, and said to Peter, surely thou art one of them, for thy speech bewrayeth thee. Then began he to curse and to swear, saying, I know not the man. And immediately, the cock crew"**
>
> *Matthew 26: 73-74*

Peter became the dean of the apostles after Jesus's crucifixion, but he doubted and gave in to negative words.

There are some situations when we may find difficulties in responding to some annoying circumstances—such as a situation when someone is pushing your buttons with irritating words. In this trying circumstance, it will not make sense to respond impulsively. What is needed is a moment or two to reflect on whether your quick reaction, if expressed, will make things better or more likely worse. It is not by might (power of your words) that can calm inflaming situations but by His Spirit through Holy Spirit counsel. The Bible encourages us about when to speak when to remain silent, and why self-talk matters too. Employing the right words leads to healthier relationships and the joy of seeing what God can do when he is the one who speaks. The power of words is the spiritual vehicle that conveys our thoughts and emotions.

Furthermore, it provides guidelines for making sure that our speech is constructive, healthy, healing, and peaceful.

The general advice is not to respond to another person if

(a) It would likely offend someone without having any realistic possibility either of resolving the situation or improving the relationship. It is better to let the sleeping dog lie down for some time without jeopardizing the relationship permanently. Time will tell, and Holy Spirit is your constant advisor. There is no need to risk alienating them by being more candid about or negatively evaluative of their behavior than they can handle emotionally. Some people are also quick to take offense and highly reactive to criticisms. Other people's rigidity makes it impossible for them to appreciate a differing viewpoint. If these people say or do something that incurs your displeasure, it is generally best to try to overlook it and internally find a way to resolve your immediate frustrations with them rather than confronting them squarely.

(b) It would hurt their feelings. If they turn out to have a strong personality, you will have more latitude to respond frankly, but at first, it makes sense to ponder how answering candidly might affect them. Again, conscientiously evaluating is the work of the Holy Spirit to direct you on what to say, how to say it, and when to say it. You have to pray for the divine wisdom; else you can inflame the situation with your carnal mind. It is better not to say anything if you have nothing nice to say. It is not needlessly or harshly responding to someone who has acted in a way that, at the moment has made you uncomfortable.

It would make you seem defensive, closed-minded, or even cantankerous. If someone is offering you constructive criticisms, it may be important to put your ego aside and conscientiously assess their viewpoint. In some situations, it will be much better to remain silent, listen attentively to the Holy Spirit, and only then give a response (if at all). If you cannot resist the immediate impulse to defend yourself, you may miss out on a valuable opportunity to learn something significant about yourself.

(c) It would only further intensify someone's anger. When someone is far too fired up to listen rationally to anything, it will be very smart not to respond to him/her. Any response will probably be premature and serve only to make matters worse because it is likely to be misconstrued as an interruption, as though you are not really listening or taking the person seriously. In such cases —if there is to be any hope of ultimately resolving (through the Holy Spirit) the situation— it will be necessary to devote all your attention to hearing someone out and giving them every chance to fully spill out their grievances. Only then might they be open to hearing your contrasting viewpoint. Also, it is important to avoid any knee-jerk, defensive reaction that will probably heighten the individual's animosity. If someone is abusive and engages in the use of vulgarity the best advice is to calm yourself down during such confrontation. If you impulsively react to him/her without divine understanding, something of the dynamic behind their vocal ferocity, such a response may only worsen matters.

(d) It would only intensify your own anger. Following your impulse to attack a person who upsets you is only likely to exacerbate things. When things flare up with the total control of the Holy Spirit, your better judgment may be seriously compromised, and you can react in ways you will later regret. It is better to hold your tongue and do whatever is required to calm yourself than blindly follow an impulse to retaliate against the person who provoked you. It is simply impossible to respond judiciously in circumstances where you are feeling so disturbed that you are on the verge of losing it. The advice here is to meditate on the word of God and endeavor to evaluate the rationality of what is going on between your ears.

(e) It would dignify or give credence to a spiteful individual trying to degrade you. There is no good reason to respond to anyone whose prime motive is to taunt you. Internet snipers, for instance, can hurt you only with your consent. Ironically, your power in these instances comes from ignoring their theoretical jabs. In most cases, you are in no way obliged to respond to belligerent, non-constructive criticism. If someone is gratuitously attacking your character, it is senseless to try to defend yourself or to sneer back at them. The best spiritual tactic is to do nothing, which leaves you much less open to further onslaughts.

"Be still, and know that I am God: I will be exalted among the heathen, I will be exalted in the earth"

Psalm 46:10

(f) It could lead you to engage with someone whose goal is to ensnare you. If you get into the ring, it is virtually guaranteed that a TKO will ensue— that is, stooping to their level marks a defeat. As Mark Twain remarked, "Never argue with stupid people. They will drag you down to their level and then beat you up with their experience." If someone has already prodded you into responding to them and is pushing for a second round, it is a smart move to cut your losses and quit, recognizing that they are only goading you to partake in an ongoing exercise in futility or foolishness.

(g) It could reinforce behavior that needs to change. With few exceptions, it is typically best not to react to unruly behavior (in preschoolers or adults) but, tactically, to ignore it, especially since an active response might inadvertently strengthen the impulse. In all, it is the little voice of the Holy Spirit that will tell us what to say, how to say, and when to say it. We shall not make haste in our response when we are tested by the enemy.

"For I said in my haste, I am cut from before thine eyes; nevertheless thou heardest the voice of my supplications which I cried unto thee"

Psalm 31:22.

2. Who owns your tongue? God or Devil?

Our speech is either controlled by God or Satan. When God can speak through you, He tells you what is to say, how to say, and when to say it. In the past, before the Lord Jesus came down to die for our sins, God himself was behind our speech, but now it is the work of the Holy Spirit. Faithfulness in our speech determines whether God can speak through us or not. The Lord told Jeremiah that if he got rid of all the worthless things (impure thoughts) in his conversations, he would become God's mouth.

> ***"Therefore thus saith the Lord, if thou return, then will I bring thee again, and thou shalt stand before me: and if thou take forth the precious from the vile, thou shalt be as my mouth: let them return unto thee; but return not thou unto them. And I will make thee unto this people a fenced brazen wall: and they shall fight against thee, but they shall not prevail against thee: for I am with thee to save thee and to deliver thee, saith the Lord. And I will deliver thee out of the hand of the wicked, and I will redeem thee out of the hand of the terrible"***
>
> ***Jeremiah 15:19-21***

Therefore, if we remove all worthless speech from our daily conversation, at home and elsewhere, and speak only what is worthwhile and valuable, then God will be with us when we speak His word. We will become mouthpieces of God and vessels of honor for the Lord's service.

God was equally using Isaiah to deliver His words to accomplish God's plan.

> *"So shall my word be that goeth forth out of my mouth: it shall not return unto me void, but it shall accomplish that which I please, and it shall prosper in the thing whereto I sent it"*

> *Isaiah 55:11*

You cannot expect God to use your tongue when you preach ten percent of the gospel and allow the devil to use your tongue for ninety percent. Many people and workmen of God follow this model and have destroyed their ministries by the careless use of their tongue. Therefore, either life can come forth from your tongues, or you can kill people or yourself (physically and spiritually) with it *(Proverbs 18:21)*.

> *"A wholesome tongue is a tree of life: but perverseness therein is a breach in the spirit"*

> *Proverbs 15:4*

There are two contrasting fires related to the tongue, mentioned in the New Testament. One is the *"tongue of fire"* that fell on the disciples' heads when they were baptized in the Holy Ghost. The other is the *"tongue set on fire by hell"* Everybody, either a believer or non-believer has chosen one or will choose one.

> *"And there appeared unto them cloven tongues like as of fire, and it sat upon each of them.*

And they were filled with the Holy Ghost, and began to speak with other tongues, as the Spirit gave them utterance"

Acts 2:3-4

and

"And the tongue is a fire, a world of iniquity: so is the tongue among our members, that it defileth the whole body, and setteth on fire the course of nature: and it is set on fire of hell"

James 3:6

Who owns your tongue today? God or Satan. Let God control your tongue through what you get in your heart. To control our tongue, we must first control our hearts. Jesus said that the mouth speaks out that which fills the heart.

"O generation of Vipers, how can ye being evil, speak good things? For out of the abundance of the heart, the mouth speaketh. A good man out of the good treasure of the heart bringeth forth good things: and an evil man out of the evil treasure bringeth forth evil things. But I say unto you, that every idle word that men shall speak, they shall give account thereof in the day of judgment. For by thy words thou shalt be justified, and by thy words, thou shalt be condemned"

Matthew 12: 34-37

Thus, we must take care of our heart first, in order to control our tongue. If dirty water is coming from a tap, it is because the tank from which the water is coming is dirty. Now, the tank must be cleaned first. Then clean water alone will come through the tap. We always speak from the thoughts that fill our hearts. So if we meditate much on the word of God, our thoughts will automatically come from us. However, if our hearts are filled with irritation against people, then that is what will spill out.

We should never speak (or write) if we sense a disturbance in our hearts—we need the peace of God to be a referee or an umpire in our hearts.

> *"And let the peace of God rule in your hearts, to which also ye are called in one body; and be ye, thankful. Let the word of Christ dwell in you richly in all wisdom; teaching and admonishing one another in psalms and hymns and spiritual songs, singing with grace in your hearts to the Lord"*

> *Colossians 3: 15-16*

Whenever we lose our peace, it is the referee or umpire blowing the whistle to remind us that a foul has been committed somewhere. Upon assessment, we must clean the foul before proceeding further. Again, whenever any disturbing thoughts cross your mind, it is proper to take those thoughts from the Lord in prayer, again and again. His furnace will purify all human irritation and anger. Finally, what you speak out are the purified words that God wants you to speak—even if they are words of rebuke.

> **"The words of the Lord are pure words: as silver tried in a furnace of earth, purified seven times"**
>
> **Psalm 12: 6**

After all these processes, God will support you and your ministry. The same process must be repeated when writing an email or a letter to correct someone.

3. Mind Your Words:

As believers of Jesus Christ, we must be careful that we do not speak against other religions and their idols by name. We must not make fun of them. Jesus never spoke about such matters during his ministry on earth. He was mainly concerned about the evil within people who claimed to know the true God.

When Paul was in Ephesus preaching on the uncompromised truth of Jesus Christ, his message was on Christ only, and not on other gods in the city. The people and the mayor realized that Paul and his partner did not denounce the great goddess Diana *(Acts 19:27)*. Furthermore, they did not denounce the false gods that the people in Ephesus were worshipping. He focused on a positive message on how to win souls for Jesus Christ. The divine wisdom helped them to move away from the negative message of criticizing their false gods and idols.

Once a person comes to Christ, the Lord Himself will convict them to get rid of all their idols. When Paul was delivered, he got rid of all his idols.

We need divine wisdom all the time so that we may not burden ourselves with unnecessary offenses. We may not know what to say, how to say, and when to say it. The general advice is to not criticize any religion, or its beliefs, or its practices. This is not our message to the world. We preach "CHRIST ONLY"—Jesus Christ crucified for our sins, raised from the dead, alive in heaven today, and returning soon to judge the world. Every believer has the responsibility of calling everyone to turn from their sins to Jesus Christ as their Lord and Savior. In the process, we are not to coerce anybody to come to the Lord. God has given everybody their free will on the question of accepting Jesus Christ. God has the power to force everybody to worship Him, but He will not do that. He will not be a fair God. Similarly, we must give people freedom too. When people genuinely receive Christ into their lives, the other false gods and idols in their lives will all gradually fall away over time because the Holy Spirit will convict them of sins.

Our calling is to proclaim Jesus Christ as the only way and Savior of the world *(John 14:6)*. Many religions and related belief systems get offended by making Christ the only way to heaven. If Christ is going to judge the world, then He must be the only way to salvation. We must equally speak against sin and judge ourselves and expose hypocrisy in our midst in the first place.

Many zealous Christians at times make name-calling and jokes about other religions in their prayers unnecessarily. There is no need to do that because God did not send His only Son into the world to condemn the world but to save it.

> **"For God sent not his Son into the world to condemn the world; but that the world through him might be saved. He that believeth on him is not condemned: but he that believeth not is condemned already, because he hath not believed in the name of the only begotten Son of God"**
>
> *John 3:17-18*

Our calling is to follow Jesus' example, and so we must preach "CHRIST ONLY" and always seek to save others, not condemn them.

4. Get real with the Word

Biblical patriarchs such as Sarai, Moses, Naomi, David, and Peter struggled with their words. What to say and how to say it, and what not to say, and when it is best to remain silent. What to do when you have said something you wish you could eat it back. Our speech to the internet with friends, co-workers, family, and strangers as well as in private, public, online, and prayer matters. We have to honor God with our words no matter how politically correct we want to be.

You are a better person when you are speaking faith. Your thoughts direct your words, and your words direct your life. Guard your heart and guard your words.

For many believers whose mouths have not been purged by the fire of the Holy Ghost, your tongue may be getting you into trouble. The tongue is the most powerful generator of either the negative or the positive—good or evil occurrences so, if any human organ needs deliverance, it is the tongue.

Almost all God's powers given to man can be traced to the spoken words of Jesus. The words that I speak unto you are spirit and life *(John 6:63).* When we speak God's words, they carry spirit and life. When we speak Satan's words, they carry bondage and death.

Our lives are a product of our confession. You can use your tongue to steal, kill and destroy yourself or others. That is why the Scriptures quote, *"And the tongue is a fire, a world of iniquity" (James 3:6).*

Words are creatures and things. They have energy and spiritual power. What you say becomes somebody or you. Challenges are opportunities to demonstrate your faith in the lord and prove His word. The word in your mouth is a creative force. It can spring forth miracles. God's word created everything. Use faith-based words to flame your world.

5. Final Thoughts

We need divine wisdom to calm down extenuating circumstances and divine understanding to walk away from evil.

The challenge for believers is to strive for the Holy Spirit to help us realize God's plan in our lives. James chapter 3 lays it out for us.

> ***"For in many things, we offend all. If any man offends not in word, the same is a perfect man, and able also to bridle the whole body"***
>
> ***James 3:2***

For those whose mouths have not been purged by the fire of the Holy Ghost, your tongue can put you into trouble. You cannot ambush the enemy with no tongues (the inability to flow with the Holy Spirit). The tongue is regarded as the most powerful generator of either the negative or the positive (good or evil occurrences). Therefore, if any human organ needs deliverance at all, it is the tongue, and they that love it shall eat the fruit thereof. Sometimes, it is smart to play dumb and keep your mouth shut.

All believers should stop negative talk. We are created to talk and see positively. However, Satan has been pushing negative and conflicting messages in our minds since the fall of man. Stop talking about your feelings, wants, and frustrations, and focus on your future in Christ Jesus. You must talk about things that will increase the

Lord and decrease you. Do not speak from your heart because, above all things, it is desperately wicked. Do not trust your heart, especially when you are angry.

At times the Holy Spirit will convict you to speak out. It happened to me when I was closing up this chapter. It was the truth, but it sounded politically incorrect. ***"But his word was in mine heart as a burning fire shut up in my bones, and I was weary with forbearing, and I could not st**ay"* *Jeremiah 29:9b*

Like Jeremiah, the Holy Spirit made me spill out the truth, but it hurt some friends.

6. Let's Pray

Father God, I *[insert your name about here]* want to reflect your love and grace each time I open my mouth to speak. Help me to slow my tongue before I say something hurtful that can have lasting consequences. When I fall short, help me to be quick to seek forgiveness and reconciliation. Let God's word take me along the right path. Father Lord, help me, *[insert your name about here]* to choose one of the Scripture verses in today's devotion and work to memorize it. Help me not to go down the slippery slope of speaking too soon and too much.

Lord, remove fear from me, *[insert your name about here]* and let me rest in the peace of God. Father, let the Holy Spirit season my utterances for me every day. Holy Spirit, breathe peace and life into me all the time. Let the words of my mouth and the meditation of my heart be acceptable in your sight, O Lord, my strength, my refuge, my rock, and my redeemer.

Father Lord, let the blood of Jesus wash all the satanic acid on my tongue. I *[insert your name about here]* am a man of unclean mouth purge my mouth with the Holy Ghost fire as you did for prophet Isaiah.

I decree the exit of the following spirits from my life in the name of Jesus: Lying, speech perversion, exaggeration, stammering, talkativeness, nagging, and murmuring. Let the fire of God purge my tongue from the contamination of evil consumption, evil vows, sexual pervasion, evil kiss, and verbal concoction. I cut myself off from every spirit of tongue and venomous speech. Lord, give me a wholesome tongue. Lord, make my *[insert your name about here]* voice, the voice of deliverance, healing, power, solution, and life.

Let my tongue become an instrument of the glory of God, in the name of Jesus. Lord, loosen my tongue and use it for your glory. Let my *[insert your name about here]* tongue guide the sad and the lonely. Lord, baptize my tongue with love and fire. Lord, let my tongue strengthen those who are discouraged. Lord, let my tongue bring straying sheep back to the vineyard. Lord, let my tongue tell others about your glory and love. Anoint my mouth to preach your word in spirit and truth.

Jesus Christ defeated the whole kingdom of darkness and won an overwhelming victory by disarming principalities and powers at the cross. Jesus is the victor. He is a mighty conqueror. Jesus triumphed over all his foes, and he has given me complete victory over every foe in my life. This includes a victory over Satan, demons, and the whole kingdom of darkness, as well as victory over all works of darkness, including witches, and wizards. Therefore, Satan, demons, witches, and warlocks, you have absolutely no power and no authority over me. Lord Jesus, let your kingdom come in the power of the Holy Spirit and glory of God. I *[insert your name about here]* seal this prayer with the precious blood of the Great Shepherd of the sheep and with thanksgiving. Amen.

Chapter 7

Tattoo Mania: Are they cool for Christians?

"You shall not make any cuttings in your flesh for the dead, nor tattoo any marks on you. I am the Lord"

Leviticus 19:28

"All things are lawful for me, but all things are not helpful. All things are lawful for me, but I will not be brought under the power of any"

1 Corinthians 6:12

"But take heed lest by any means this liberty of yours become a stumbling block to them that are weak"

1 Corinthians 8:9

"In whom also ye are circumcised with the circumcision made without hands, in putting off the body of the sins of the flesh by the circumcision of Christ"

Colossians 2:11

"But ye are a chosen generation, a royal priesthood, an holy nation, a peculiar people; that ye should shew forth the praises of him who hath called you out of darkness into his marvelous light"

1 Peter 2:9

"And I will power unto my two witnesses, and they shall prophesy a thousand two hundred and threescore days, clothed in sackcloth. These are the two olive trees and the two candlesticks standing before the God of the earth"

Revelation 11: 3-4

1. Introduction

Tattoos have become an immensely popular fashion statement among youth these days. Today, people regard tattoos as a way of asserting one's personality and a marker of their identity. Exposure to Western culture has transformed youth immensely as love for tattoos has taken hold. Tattoos have also become influenced by international music stars and sports heroes who often display elaborate body art. The tattoo was until recently reserved for the heavy metal rocker or biker, a criminal, and the social outcast of society. But today, tattoo glamorously appears everywhere and anywhere. It is the latest fashion craze. Within the last decade, tattooing has become widespread. Tattoos are found on movie stars such as Julia Roberts, Halle Berry, Drew Berrymore, and Bruce Willis. Music stars such as Jon Bon Jovi, Eminem, Beyoncé, and many favorite stars such as Britney Spears. It is no surprise that over 45% of NBA players have at least one tattoo. Even in the conservative Golf World, both Tiger Woods and Lee Trevino have tattoos. People are keen on getting different portraits, patterns, and name initials, etc., tattooed on their visible body parts. Many of them are going in for cover-up tattoos to get rid of their old designs.

A tattoo has now acquired different connotations—it is used to profess love, to honor the dead, and sometimes nothing. Since a tattoo is going to be a part of them, they might as well know it in and out. Not all clients understand the meaning of what they are getting on their bodies. Some do know the story in and out as well. It is a universally acknowledged fact that tattoos are powerful tools of self-expression,"

Tattoos have certainly outgrown their bad reputation. We no longer live in a world where tattoos are only seen on mob bosses, zealous, religious practitioners, and hardened criminals. Today's society has slowly accepted tattoos as a work of art. It comes as no surprise that practically anyone from any walk of life has at least one. The following statistics prove this point: World-wide tattoos are more of the Western culture than the rest of the World. Italy=48%, Sweden=47%, USA=46%, Australia=43%, Argentina=43%, Spain=42%, Denmark=41%, UK=40%, are the percentages of the population permanently-inked the skin in 2018. Related statistics are as follows: 36% of US citizens aged 18-29 have at least one tattoo. 72% of tatted adults have tattoos that are hidden by their clothing. In 2012, around 45 million people (21%) in America alone had one or more tattoos, 35% of United Kingdom citizens aged 30-39 have tattoos, 30% of US college graduates have tattoos, 11% of people with tattoos in the United States belong in the age range of 50-64 years old; 15% of men and 13% of women in the US have tattoos; 36% of the US Armed Forces, including military veterans, have tattoos; Tattoos seem to be more popular with people who attained higher levels of education (32%) compared to those with lower education levels (26%); With 38% of adults aged 30-39 being tatted, older millennial are the most likely people to get a tattoo.

The focus of this chapter is to promote Holy Spirit-filled Christians over tattooed Christians. The trademarks of Christians are the blood of the Lamb in the form of invisible lights in front and behind true Christians, which are sanctified by the Holy Spirit. Christians receive invisible tattoos initiated to us by our Lord Jesus Christ through the Holy Spirit's power. Our names are tattooed on the Lord's hands and in his blood. They are invisible tattoos. You cannot see them with your naked eyes. We cannot defy our bodies with tattoos because they are the temples of God. If we defy our bodies with tattoos, we are no longer the temples of God. We become the temples of Satan and lose our invisible tattoos and eternal salvation. As Christians, we bear in our bodies the mark of the blood of the Lamb.

In the natural, people have tattoos on their bodies to remind them of some event or experience in their lives, whether positive or negative. Tattoos are a reminders and they are a statements. I believe the Lord wants us to give Him permission to remove the tattoos on our souls that remind us of the pain that was inflicted on us.

One of the things hidden in the tattoo is un-forgiveness. It is not obvious because the enemy's scheme is to keep you in pain. Lest Satan should take advantage of us, for we are not ignorant of his devices **(2 Corinthians 2:11).** When the Lord removes the tattoo of that memory, the un-forgiveness will be revealed and healed.

Another thing hidden behind the tattoo is pride. The tattoo reminds us of an experience that happened to us, so we do not let anyone ever do that to us again. Anger is the anesthesia that numbs the pain and becomes a breeding ground for pride. Pride in one of its forms is self-protection, and once the tattoo is removed, the Lord will become your God— is our refuge and strength, a well-proven help in trouble **(Psalm 46:1)**

Can all those who have tattoos be saved? Jesus came for the sinners and not the self-righteous, so we must not put down those with tattoos because almost all people who came to the Lord as were sinners. God is kind to the ungrateful and the wicked, and we all have been ungrateful and wicked now and in the past. Tattooed folks deserve love and patience. Instead of putting people down as sinners, we must care for people who are at the fringes of society. Jesus is the friend of sinners, so we must follow him without questions. God loves us and desires more than anything that we love and obey. He desires above all our total obedience unto eternal life. He also desires our willingness to receive his Son, our Lord Jesus Christ *(John 1:12).*

2. Arguments for and against increasing Demand for Tattoos

God told the Israelites then and is also telling us today that "Ye shall not make any cuttings in your flesh for the dead, nor print, nor tattoo, any marks upon you: I am the Lord" *(Leviticus 19:28).* First, this was the law then and the law now because it ends by *"I am the Lord"* in the present tense. The background of this law was that of Israel, after being rescued from slavery, was between Egypt and Canaan. The argument for tattoos on this particular verse in Leviticus is that historical evidence suggests that tattooing the body parts of women associated with fertility (breasts, thighs, and abdomen) was believed to be a good luck charm to protect the birthing process. Women also frequently had imprints of the fertility goddess, Bes, which seems to support this claim. Tattooing has been around for thousands of years. It has a rich history in Eurasia, Japan, Egypt, and many various cultures have had their own tattoo traditions, ranging from rubbing cuts and other wounds with ashes to hand-pricking the skin to insert dyes. In general, tattoos have served as rites of passage, marks of status and rank, decorations for bravery, sexual lures and marks of fertility, pledges of love, punishment, protection, and as the marks of outcasts, slaves, and convicts. In this passage in Leviticus, God was warning Israelites to stay from the common religious practices of the surrounding cultures that would include eating bloody meat, fortune telling, certain hair cut related to the priests of false cults, cutting or marking the body for dead relatives, cultic prostitution and consulting psychics. All these practices would lead God's beloved people away from Him and toward false gods. The book of Leviticus contains mostly the priestly code and a lot of ceremonial rules and regulations. Apostle Paul reveals this in his letter to the Church in Galatia.

> **"Wherefore the law was our Schoolmaster to bring us unto Christ, that we might be justified by faith, But after that faith comes, we are no longer under the Schoolmaster"**
>
> **Galatians 3:24-25**

Again, the Lord forbids his people and warns us to come out from slavery and bondage practices in the world system.

> **"But ye are a chosen generation, a royal priesthood, a holy nation, a peculiar people; that ye should shew forth the praises of him who hath called you out of darkness into his marvelous light"**
>
> **1 Peter 2:9**

Throughout history until now, tattooing and piercing have always been condemned by Bible-believing Christians. The simple truth is that tattoos come from hell. A tattoo is a seducing device of the Enemy to steal, kill and destroy millions. It does not matter what kind of tattoo you have. Even if it is the cross of Jesus, small or big— a tattoo is a tattoo. Satan will deceitfully mark you for hell if you disobey the Word of God *(Leviticus 19:28).*

Many churchgoers argue that there is no biblical mandate and little cultural taboo concerning tattoos. To them, self-righteous legalism against tattoos will not do anything good for the church. Legalistic support for tattoos comes from **Leviticus 19:27**, the text before the main text against tattoos, **Leviticus 19:28.** Why is it that the shaving of head and beard (**Leviticus 19:27** is not upheld with urgency as tattooing of the body? **Leviticus 19:28.** The counterargument is that the marks on the skin are mentioned in several verses in both the New and the Old Testaments but not the shaving of the head and beard.

> *"And he causeth all, both small and great, rich and poor, free and bond, to receive a mark in their right hand, or in their foreheads: And that no man might buy or sell, save he that the mark, or the name of the beast, or the number of his name"*
>
> *Revelation 13:16-17*

Moreover, the following biblical verses support the mark on the skin *(Revelation 14:9, 11: 16:2; 19:20; 20:4).*

We need to be wise in the exercise of our freedom and not cause anyone to stumble, especially a weaker Christian. Again, Paul reminds us that we are free, and because of our sanctification in Christ, whatever we touch becomes sanctified. The meat sacrificed to idols does not hurt a Christian when he consumes it. However, Paul did not carry tattooing logic to the issue of meat openly sacrificed to idols. Therefore, tattooing remains a law of paramount concern to God as referenced in the Old Testament and several times in the New Testament. Accepting tattoos now may make it easier to receive the mark of the beast. This is a slow and deceitful device of the enemy to steal, kill and take millions to perdition. It must be noted that getting COVID-19 vaccination is not a prelude to the mark of the beast (666) because many prophecies are not yet fulfilled before the emergence of the beast and the false prophet. Do not try to hurry up the Lord's Second Coming calendar. Even the angels in Heaven do not know the date and the time of His coming.

The common belief among tattooed folks is that tattoos make them bold and fearless. Thus, the tattoos protect them from evil spirits. To some, tattoos give them platforms to broadcast who they are and to have a chance to stand out, especially those in show business, professional athletes, and related celebrities. And to some, marks of status and rank, sexual lures and pledges of love, and the marks of an outcast, slaves, and convicts. Many get them for symbolic meanings and strictly for the looks but end up regrettably getting them in the first place. Nobody with a tattoo or body piercing is innocent. Your innocence or naivety in this matter is no excuse. The price you pay spiritually, whether you know it or not is for life if you do not have a change of mind to remove it. The price for removing a tattoo and the complications with surgery may not be worth it in the long run. The evil connotations can hurt you spiritually, so get deliverance by renouncing the spirits behind the tattoos. Christian tattoo is plain stupidity because moral commandments reiterated in the New Testament are based on the character of God. Some pastors and preachers have tattoos as devices to draw people with tattoos to the Lord. Wrong! Jesus loves all sinners, but He did not become a tax collector (a sinner) to draw Zacchaeus to himself *(Luke 19:1-10).*

> *"For rebellion is as the sin of witchcraft, and stubbornness is as iniquity and idolatry"*
>
> *1 Samuel 15:23a*

Tattoos are by and large associated with gangs who arguably worship false gods of violence, drug use, and sexual immorality. Tattooing is a form of rebellion against the character of God.

> *"Sanctify yourselves, therefore, and be ye holy: for I am the Lord your God"*
>
> *Leviticus 20:7*

Today, our world is full of hatred, wickedness, and lovers of themselves more than God, and violence as a result of rebellion. The wicked shall do wickedly, and none of the wicked shall understand. But the wise shall understand *(Daniel 12:10).*

> *"Now the Spirit speaketh expressly, that in the latter times some shall depart from the faith, giving heed to seducing spirits, and doctrines of devils. Speaking lies in hypocrisy, having their conscience seared with a hot iron"*

1 Timothy 4: 1-2

Tattooed folks do not own themselves. Their lives can be taken from them at God's will, so why do they brag off with their tattooed bodies. We were all bought at a price over 2000 years ago by our Lord Jesus Christ, so we have to glorify God in our bodies and in our spirit, which is God's *(1 Corinthians 6: 19-20).* Moreover, your body is the temple of the Holy Spirit who is in you, who you have from God. You cannot defy your body with tattoos. Once your body is defied by tattoos, you are exposed to diseases such as Aids, Hepatitis B, Hepatitis C, Tetanus, syphilis, and even tuberculosis. The internet is loaded with information about the risk factors associated with tattoos. People try to rationalize things and say it is okay and cool to get a tattoo. The question is should you get it?

> *All things are lawful for me, but all things are not expedient: all things are lawful for me, but all things edify not"*

1 Corinthians 10:23

Yes, you are allowed to do anything, but not everything encourages your spiritual growth. Christians are expected to get away from all forms of tattoos because we are not part of the world and should not love the things of the world.

> *"Love not the world, neither the things that are in the world. If any man love the world, the love of the Father is not in him, For all that is in the world, the lust of the flesh, and the*

lust of the eyes, and the pride of life, is not of the Father, but is of the world. And the world passeth away, and the lust thereof: but he that doeth the will of God abideth forever"

1 John 2: 15-17

Do you want a tattoo because everyone has one? Do you think tattoos are cool? It is hard living in today's world with all the temptations, but you do not have to prove to anyone that you are cool with tattoos.

"And be not conformed to this world: but be ye transformed by the renewing of your mind, that ye may prove what is that good, and acceptable, and perfect will of God"

Romans 12:2

You are a child of the King and not a slave. Examine your motives for getting a tattoo and say, I know, I don't want one. God made man in His own image and in His likeness. **(Genesis 1:26). A** man was the only created being made in the image of God. You have been made in the image of God. No matter what is happening to you, God is your daddy. Jesus is telling us to grow up like our Daddy in Heaven. Everything we do and say should reflect our creator because we are created in His image. We are to be light and shine to glorify our Father, who is in Heaven.

"Let your light so shine before me, that they may see your works, and glorify your Father which is in Heaven"

Matthew 5:16

3. Spiritual Tattoos

The anointing of the Holy Spirit within our bodies and the Spirit of the Lord brings fear to those who do not have the tattoo (Spirit) of the Lord. When the Spirit of the Lord departed from King Saul, a distressing spirit from the Lord troubled him, and he feared David.

"And Saul was yet the more afraid of David, and Saul became David's enemy continually"

1 Samuel 18:29

A true Christian, who has the Spirit of the Lord (tattooed by the Spirit of the Lord), is more fearful than the children of disobedience who have worldly tattoos. The tattoo of the Lord presents formidable fear to Satan, demons, and his children.

"I will send my fear before thee, and will destroy all the people to whom thou shalt come, and I will make all thine enemies turn their backs unto thee"

Exodus 23:27

In the reign of King Herod, everybody, including the king, knew that John the Baptist had the Spirit or tattoo of the Lord, and they feared him.

> ***"For Herod feared John, knowing that he was a just and a holy, and observed him: and when he heard him, he did many things, and heard him gladly"***
>
> ***Mark 6:20***

If the fear of the Lord does not go before and behind you, check your Christian life. In the book of Acts, we observed the people who claimed to possess the Spirit or tattoo of the Lord but under false pretenses. The most vivid accounts of such false anointing of the Lord are as follows: The Elymas, the sorcerer called Bar-Jesus, and the seven sons of Sceva.

> ***"But Elymas, the sorcerer (for so is his name by interpretation) withstood them, seeking to turn away the deputy from the faith. Then Saul, who also is called Paul, filled with the Holy Spirit, set his eyes on him. And said 'O full of subtilty and all mischief, thou enemy of all righteousness, wilt thou not cease to pervert the right ways of the Lord? And now, behold, the hand of the Lord is upon thee, and thou shalt be blind, not seeing the sun for a season. And immediately there fell on him a mist and darkness, and he went about seeking some to lead him by the hand"***

Acts 13:8-11

This false Jesus suffered blindness in the end because he was a phony and did not have the true anointing or tattoo of the Lord. You will pay a heavy price for faking to possess the Spirit of the Lord.

> ***"Then certain of the vagabond Jews, exorcists took it upon them to call over them which had evil spirits the name of the Lord Jesus, saying, we adjure you by Jesus whom Paul preacheth. And there were seven sons of one sceva, a Jew, and the priests, which do so. And the evil spirit answered and said, Jesus, I know, and Paul,I know, but who are ye? And the man in whom the evil spirit was, leaped on them, overcame them, and prevailed against them so that they fled out of that house naked and wounded. And this was known to all the Jews and Greeks also dwelling at Ephesus, and fear fell on them all, and the name of the Lord Jesus was magnified"***

Acts 19: 13-17

If you claim to have the true Spirit of the Lord, we shall know you by your fruits in the short term (immediately) or in the long term. The baptism of the Holy Spirit can be visualized as the Lord's tattoos on our bodies, but it does not show on our physical bodies as those with physical tattoos. Even more so, if you do not have the tattoo of the Lord and you claim falsely, you will be punished now and then. There are many false pastors and prophets who are falsely claiming the anointing of the Holy Spirit; however, they are not. Satan can also anoint his people to do miracles, but you will know them by their fruits. Are you sure you have the true tattoo of the Lord?

We live in a period in which small and great, rich and poor, black and white, male and female, possess tattoos in various parts of their bodies as signs of the demons that control them. Some receive tattoos because of peer pressure but do not understand the significance of these tattoos. Why are tattoos continually becoming popular with people from all walks of life? They are the children of disobedience who have disobeyed the commandments of God. The scriptures have warned us against the use of indelible marks on our bodies *(Leviticus 19:28)*. Tattoos or indelible marks are signs of evil or satanic worship. The first person to receive a mark on his body was Cain. We know the story of how he killed his little brother Abel because of jealousy in Genesis.

> *"And the Lord said to him, therefore, whosoever slayeth Cain, vengeance shall be taken on him sevenfold. And the Lord set a mark upon Cain, lest any finding him should kill him"*
>
> *Genesis 4:15*

Generally, tattooed people are cowards because they use the physical markings on their bodies as signs of valor. Note that the righteous are as bold as a lion *(Proverbs 28:1)*. The righteous have a tattoo within his body from the Holy Spirit. Satan is a counterfeit, and his counterfeit of the Holy Spirit's baptism is the physical tattoos on the bodies of his children.

If you have a tattoo, your master is Satan. You cannot become a true Christian and keep tattoos on your body. Light and darkness do not meet. Separate yourself and come out among them by deliverance through the renouncing of the demon(s) behind your tattoos.

> ***"Wherefore come out from among them, and be ye separate, saith the Lord, and touch not the unclean thing, and I will receive you"***
>
> ***2 Corinthians 6:17***

You do not need a tattoo to give you a mark of bravery. It is the Holy Spirit's baptism that gives you power and authority. When the Holy Spirit's fire is upon you, you will be filled with new wine, and Satan, his demons, and the children of disobedience will be afraid of you. When a Christian is given the Lord's tattoo, the presence of the Lord goes before and behind him/her. The presence of the Lord in our lives gives us strength and boldness to do exploits.

> ***"And such as do wickedly against the covenant shall be corrupt by flatteries: but the people that know their God shall be strong and do exploits"***
>
> ***Daniel 11:32***

> ***"And the Spirit of the Lord came mightily upon him (Samson), and he tore the Lion apart as one would have torn apart a young goat, though he had nothing in his hand. But he did not tell his father or his mother what he had done"***

Judges 14:6

Tattooed men and women must understand that it is not the tattooed skin that matters but the presence of the Lord that works miracles in their lives. When the Spirit of the Lord departed from Samson, he could no longer do any mighty deed. When the Lord's anointing left him, Samson became an ordinary man. Samson's tattoos were in his long hair. When they cut off the hair, and he was totally powerless.

> ***"But the Philistines took him and put out his eyes and brought him down to Gaza, and bound him with fetters of brass: and he did grind in the prison house:***

Judges 16:21

However, the presence of the Lord can stay with us continually.

> ***The Lord blesses thee and keeps thee. The Lord makes His face shines upon thee, and be gracious to thee. The Lord lifts up His countenance upon thee, and gives thee peace"***

Numbers 6:24-26

The Spirit of the Lord stayed with these saints forever; Abraham, Isaac, Jacob, Joseph, Moses, Elijah, Isaiah, Jeremiah, and many more.

> ***The Lord our God be with us, as he was with our fathers. Let Him not leave us nor forsake us"***

185

1 Kings 8:57

There are cases where the presence of the Lord may be hidden from us. We cannot see God's presence in our lives unless the Lord opens our eyes through visions or dreams. Like Gideon, we may be spiritual giants but not know it unless the Lord reveals Himself to us.

> ***"And he answered, fear not, for they that be with us are more they that be with them. And Elisha prayed, and said, Lord, I pray thee, open his eyes, that he may see. And the Lord opened the eyes of the young man, and he saw and behold, the mountain was full of horses and chariots of fire round about Elisha"***

2 Kings 6: 16-17

Furthermore, we have instances where the Spirit of the Lord or the Lord's tattoos in our lives can be discerned by those with and without physical tattoos.

> ***"And Elijah answered and said to the captain of fifty, if I am a man of God, then let fire come down from heaven and consume thee and fifty. And there came down from heaven, and consumed him and his fifty"***

2 Kings 1:10

Another scripture reveals the Lord's tattoos in his saints.

186

"And when the sons of the prophets which were to view at Jericho, saw him, they said, the Spirit of Elijah rests on Elisha. And they came to meet him, and bowed themselves to the ground before him"

2 Kings 2: 15

Tattooed folks usually boast of their physical markings over the tattooed-less people, but they are easily overpowered by those with the Lord's tattoos or the Spirit of Lord. There is no power in tattoos, but the real power is in the Lord's Spirit. The tattoos on the children of disobedience signify particular demons and what they can do for them. However, they fail to deliver their services when they meet the children of God. We can see this account in the book of Acts when Paul and Silas met the woman with the spirit of divination.

"And this did she many days. But Paul, being grieved, turned and said to the spirit, I command thee in the name of Jesus Christ to come out of her. And he came out the same hour. And when her masters saw that the hope of their gains was gone, they caught Paul and Silas and drew them into the marketplace to the rulers"

Acts 16: 18-19

Similarly, Jesus of Nazareth, in many occasions, rebuked demons and freed those possessed by demons.

> *"And devils also came out of many, crying out and saying, "Thou art Christ, the Son of God". And he, rebuking them, suffered them not to speak, for they knew that he was Christ"*

> *Luke 4:41*

The anointing of the Lord (tattoo) breaks yoke and bondage. The Spirit of the Lord will rest on the elect of God and those who obey his Word. Obedience to God makes you a candidate to receive Holy Spirit tattoo and do exploits.

> *"And I will give power unto my two witnesses, and they shall prophesy a thousand two hundred and threescore days, clothed in sackcloth. These are the two olive trees, and the two candlesticks standing before the God of the earth. And if any man will hurt them, fire proceedeth out of their mouth, and devoureth their enemies: and if any man will hurt them, he must in this manner be killed"*

> *Revelation 11: 3-5*

The two witnesses are highly anointed and tattooed by the Lord to prophesy to his people in the tribulation era. The anointing of the Lord on them will prepare them for miracles and encouragement to those who will miss the rapture.

In the tribulation, people who love God will leave Babylon and step across the line to God's side. Conversely, people who refuse to surrender to the truth will have no other option but to join the devil. In choosing his church, people will receive his mark, which will allow them (through buying and selling) to obtain the necessities of life. The mark of the beast is (a tattoo showing either the literal number **666** or the name of the devil) will indicate church membership in the devil's church (universal church or World religion). Consider the outcome: if people take the side of God, they will experience the devil's wrath. If people take the side of the devil, they will also experience God's wrath. Surely, this will be a time of wrath for everyone.

4. *Get Real with the Word of God*

God has given every man his free will, and it is unfortunate that many live in uncleanness, in the lust of their hearts to dishonor their bodies among themselves (Tattoos). Tattoos have become more popular than ever because Satan and his demons know that the Lord's Second Coming is drawing near. These demons are enticing and seducing men and women (rich or poor, black or white, small or big), especially Christians from apostate-thinking states to tattooing. Once they get the bodies of Christians, their spirits will naturally succumb to their tricks and traps.

The tattoo is a mark of disobedience because God tells us not to mark our bodies **(Leviticus 19:28)**. I am not judging tattoo folks, but you will surely come under the judgment of God. Get deliverance by renouncing the spirit behind the tattoos and getting a real tattoo from the Lord. Tattooed folks usually boast of their physical markings over others, but they are easily overpowered by those with the Lord's tattoos or the Spirit of the Lord. There is no power in tattoos. Real power is in the Lord's Spirit. You do not need a tattoo to give you a mark of bravery. It is the Holy Spirit's baptism that gives you power and authority. When the Holy Spirit's fire is upon you, you will be filled with new wine, and Satan, his demons, and the children of disobedience will be afraid of you. Tattooed folks are cowards because they use physical markings on their bodies as signs of valor. The righteous are as bold as a lion.

Since we were born in the image of God, everything we do and say should reflect Him. God will not have a tattoo, so why do you have one or more? We grow up to reflect His image and character. We were created to live a life that reflects our creator. Since we have God's image, we should let our light shine before others so that they may see our good works and give glory to our Father, who is in Heaven.

The challenge most of us face is the reality that the past pain, the sin, the situation has become a tattoo on our soul. A tattoo is a constant reminder of what happened to us. For each person, that tattoo may look different, but every person knows what that tattoo reminds them of. In the natural, people have tattoos on their bodies to remind them of some event or experience in their lives, whether positive or negative. Tattoos are a reminder; and they are a statement. I believe the Lord wants us to give Him permission to remove the tattoos on our souls that remind us of the pain that was inflicted on us. Jesus says, "The Spirit of the Lord is upon me because He has anointed me to preach the gospel to the poor; He has sent me to heal the broken-hearted, to preach deliverance to the captives and recovery of sight to the blind, to set at liberty those who are bruised, such as the tattooed and skin- pierced folks."**(Luke 4:18).**

5. Final Thought:

Simply, tattoos come from hell. It is a scheme of Satan to destroy and take you to hell. Even one small tattoo is still a tattoo. It does not matter what type of tattoo it is. Even if it is of a cross of Jesus— a tattoo is a tattoo. Satan will mark you for hell if you disobey the Word of God. The Bible says in Leviticus 19:28. Ye shall not make any cuttings in your flesh for the dead, not print or make any marks upon you: I am the Lord." You do not need a tattoo to give you a mark of bravery. It is the Holy Spirit's baptism that gives you power and authority.

Let us review tattoos in light of the clarity of our mission in God and the purity of our motive with God. If tattoos are not honoring God, why are Christians having tattoos? Are we trying to provoke God or what? Our mission is to pursue God like John the Baptist, whose mission was to increase Jesus and decrease himself *(John 3:30)*. Tattooed folks draw attention to themselves and not God. They are not humble and are easily offended, legalistic, and defensive. They project themselves to the world. Their motive is self-centered (they point people to themselves instead of Jesus). Tattooed folks are all for themselves. John the Baptist, the forerunner of the Lord Jesus Christ and was considered the greatest prophet born of women. **(Matthew 11:11).**

One of the things hidden in the tattoo is un-forgiveness. It is not obvious, because it is a scheme of the enemy to keep you in pain. Lest Satan should take advantage of us, for we are not ignorant of his devices **(2 Corinthians 2:11)**. When the Lord removes the tattoo of that memory, the un-forgiveness will be revealed and healed.

Another thing hidden behind the tattoo is pride. The tattoo reminds us of an experience that happened to us, so we do not let anyone ever do that to us again. Anger is the anesthesia that numbs the pain and becomes a breeding ground for pride. Pride in one of its forms is self-protection, and once the tattoo is removed, the Lord will become your God refuge and strength, a well-proven help in trouble **(Psalm 46:1)**. There is nothing God cannot redeem. God needs to remove some tattoos from your life. Are you willing to accept the invitation of God for tattoo removal this morning, this afternoon, this evening, this night, today, or tomorrow?

6. *Let's Pray,*

Father, I ***insert your name about here*** run into your open arms. Thank you for your mercy and grace that is abundant. I can always trust you to never turn me away because you love me. In fact, you loved me so much that you sent your Son to earth to pay the price in full for my redemption and freedom. Lord, I *__insert your name about here__* have given you the permission to remove the tattoos on my soul that reminds me of the pain that was inflicted on me. The Lord is inviting me to let Him remove the tattoos on my soul, not to expose me but to heal me. Father, I *__insert your name about here__* have made mistakes and stumbled in my walk with you by choosing to have tattoos all over my body. I humbly come to you because you have asked me to always come to you when I am burdened. Lord Jesus Christ, restore and make me whole by removing all tattoos from my life. Father, as you remove my tattoos, help me to deal with un-forgiveness, pain, and pride associated with them.

Father, I know that I, *__insert your name about here,__* have not presented my body as a living sacrifice, holy and acceptable, unto you, which is my reasonable service *(Romans 12: 1).* I have been living for myself by conforming to this world with tattoos and other demonic designs. Holy Spirit, transform me by renewing my mind and getting rid of all the tattoos and satanic objects on my body. Please, forgive me for all my sins, just as I forgive others. I, *__insert your name about here,__* acknowledge the completed work of Your only begotten Son, Jesus Christ, giving his life for me on the cross. Holy Spirit, come into my life now. Grant me the riches of your glory to be strengthened with might by his Spirit in my inner man *(Ephesians 3:16).* Lord, come into my heart and be my king, my Lord, and my Savior. From this day forward, I will no longer be controlled by sin or the desire to please myself with tattoos and satanic signs, but I will follow you all the days of my life. Holy Spirit, guide me ***insert your name about here,*** into all truth about tattoos.

Open my spiritual eyes to see that heaven is my ultimate home and the world is my temporary home. Grant me the inner spiritual strength to resist temptations and control my mind. Your word never dies, and it remains the same till now. Your word is the truth and higher than your name. May God grant me wisdom and make me strong. Let me ***insert your name about here,*** abide in you forever and ever. Lord, put your mark (spiritual tattoo) on me to show that I am all yours and put your Spirit in my heart to be a guarantee for all that you have promised me ***(2 Corinthians 1:22).***

Jesus Christ defeated the whole kingdom of darkness and won an overwhelming victory by disarming principalities and powers at the cross. Jesus Christ is the victor. He is the mighty conqueror. Jesus triumphed over all his enemies, and he has given me complete victory over every foe in my life. This includes a victory over Satan, the demons, and the whole kingdom of darkness, as well as victory over all works of darkness, including witches, and wizards. Therefore, Satan, demons, witches, and warlocks, you have no absolute power and no authority over me. Lord of glory; let your kingdom come through the power of the Holy Ghost and the glory of God. I, ***insert your name about here,*** seal this prayer with the precious blood of the Great Shepherd of the sheep and with thanksgiving, Amen.

Chapter 8
Invest in the Kingdom of God.

"Lay not up for yourselves treasures upon earth, where moth and rust doth corrupt, and where thieves break through and steal. But lay up for yourselves treasures in heaven, where neither moth nor rust doth corrupt, and where thieves do not break through nor steal."

Matthew 6:19-20

"Lo, this is the man that made not God his strength, but trusted in the abundance of his riches, and strengthened himself in his wickedness"

Psalm 52:7

"And when Jesus saw that he was very sorrowful, he said, how hardly shall they that have riches enter into the kingdom of God"

Luke 18:24

"But seek ye first the kingdom of God, and His righteousness, and all these things shall be added unto you"

Matthew 6:33

"Riches and honor are with me, yea, durable riches and righteousness. My fruit is better than gold, yea than fine gold, and my revenue than choice silver"

Proverbs 8:18-19

1. Introduction:

Today, believers and unbelievers are craving for riches in the form of houses, cars, stocks, bonds, real estate, mutual funds, and many more in a hurry. When is the scramble for worldly riches going to reduce, even before and after COVID-19? It is not going to stop, but it will accelerate as we quickly approach End times. If worldly riches are temporal, why are smart people working hard all the time to accumulate wealth upon wealth? Why are few people investing in the kingdom of God with their money, time with God, spending time on the word of God, preaching and teaching to win souls for Jesus, evangelizing and building churches around the world, feeding the poor, helping the old and orphans and even with their lives? Investors are balancing their capital structure between temporal and eternal returns. It is a choice between short-term (temporal) gains in which many crave for, and long-term (eternal) gains in which very few pursue to the point of losing their lives. Satan and his minions, including Mammon, have blinded the minds of them which believe not, lest the light of the glorious gospel of Christ, who is the image of God, should shine unto them" *(2 Corinthians 4:4).* Mammon is using money and other forms of wealth to distract man's attention from his creator (God). The problem is not with riches a man owns, but man's love for them. Many rich people spend less or no time for God because they are preoccupied with the riches and the habits of riches. Wealth becomes their god, so they worship it. Listen to the conversation between Jesus and the young ruler in Luke Chapter 18.

> *"And he said, All these have I kept from my youth up. Now when Jesus heard these things, he said unto him, yet, lackest thou one thing; sell all that thou hast, and distribute unto the poor, and thou shalt have treasure in heaven: and come, follow me. And when he heard this, he was very sorrowful, for he was very rich. And when Jesus saw that he was very sorrowful, he said, how hardly shall they that have riches enter into the kingdom of God! For it is easier for a camel to go through a needle's eye, than for a rich man to enter into the kingdom of God"*
>
> *Luke 18: 21-25*

Solomon, the wisest man who ever lived, wrote of the danger of greed in Ecclesiastes.

> **"He that loveth silver shall not be satisfied with silver; nor he that loveth abundance with increase; this is also vanity"**
>
> *Ecclesiastes 5:10*

The ugly truth is that many people, including the rich, are greedy and keep accumulating wealth forever. Show me one rich man who will tell you that he has so much money that he does not need more. Not one because his desires always exceed his needs. Most people die in their quest for more money and wealth. Their focus and heart are totally away from heaven. This is why Jesus says it is hard for a rich man to go to heaven than a camel going through a needle. Many become rich, and they lose their focus on God.

The ungodly will prosper in the world system but not in the kingdom of God because the prosperity of the fool (ungodly) will destroy him.

James has warned us about the sad end of worldly riches.

> **"Go to now, ye rich men, weep and howl for your miseries that shall come upon you. Your riches are corrupted, and your garments are moth-eaten. Your gold and silver are cankered, and the rust of them shall be a witness against you and shall eat your flesh as it were fire. Ye have heaped treasure together for the last days"**
>
> *James 5:1-3*

Thus, the ungodly will gather the riches, but the just will use them in the end. Please, what counts is not the quantity of your wealth but the quality of your investments measured in terms of God's work. Every worldly investment will yield zero return in terms of God's investment scale. However, many are dying to put their lives on such meaningless investments. We have to put our money, gold, silver, time, talents, and others in the kingdom of God, where the returns are infinite. The nature of your investments on earth depends on your relationship with God through Jesus Christ. Prayers and strong fasting can bring revival on earth, where many will start investing in the kingdom of God. Oh, how glorious it will be if the rich will lay down their treasures (riches, wealth, gifts, talents, etc.) at the storehouse of God to meet the ever-growing needs of our hurting brothers and sisters. This investment has a greater return and glorifies God more than investments in the world system. The bible story of after-death events of the poor man (Lazarus) and the rich man should tell all of us that what counts is the quality of our investments on earth (sound relationship between man and his creator-----God). Many people have questioned in their minds and hearts that why do bad (ungodly) people prosper along with the godly?

> **"Behold, these are the ungodly who prosper in the world, they increase in riches"**
>
> **Psalm 73:12**

God is a merciful God who pours out blessings for all men irrespective of their religious or alternative inclinations. It rains for the godly and ungodly. Hence, prosperity is God's ability to meet the needs of mankind regardless of what those needs are. Thus, God blesses the believer as well as the unbeliever. The riskiness of your riches depends on how you use God's ability to control your riches. The prosperity of a fool (ungodly) will destroy him because he worships the riches instead of God. He also supports the bad habits associated with riches such as drinking, drugs, lusting, and excessive spending, to mention but a few. Money is not evil but it is what happens to man's heart when he gets abundant riches. If your heart turns away from God when you become rich, money becomes evil. On the other hand, if your heart turns more to God when you become rich, your money will help the kingdom of God. Often times, many rich people become victims to the god of money (Mammon). They are consumed by the abundance of riches, so they reject the giver of riches and wealth. The curse of riches is similar to the curse of good looks. You become vulnerable to Satan's attributes (pride, arrogance, and all the fruits of evil).

> ***"For the love of money is the root of all evil which while some coveted after, they have erred from the faith, and pierced themselves through with many sorrows"***
>
> ***1 Timothy 6:10***

However, if our prosperity brings us closer and closer to God, we will have eternal returns, and we will not be destroyed by riches and wealth.

"That they do good, that they be rich in good works, ready to distribute, willing to communicate. Laying up in store for themselves a good foundation against the time to come, that they may lay hold on eternal life"

1 Timothy 6:18-19

It is good to be generous when God blesses us with riches and wealth but without a deep and personal relationship with God through Jesus Christ, our generosity has no meaning in the kingdom of God. I wish Hollywood actors, politicians, kings, and Queens who have been blessed by God Almighty with riches and wealth would distribute these to the needy and always communicate with God. It is said that many of these people continue to be destroyed by riches and the habits of riches.

The orderly pursuit of worldly riches and wealth is out of balance in God's terms. The world system has reversed God's order of investments. When a man gets up from bed, he rushes to get out of the house to go to work without a short quiet time with God. He is so obsessed with his work that he hardly finds time to eat. This tight schedule which has little or no time for God and fellowmen is not only dangerous but unprofitable in the kingdom of God. He forgets the scriptures, which says,

"What does it profit a man if he gains the whole world and loses his life, or what shall a man give in exchange for his soul?"

Matthew 16:26

I know many people who get up early in the morning, leave the house for work, and will not get back home until midnight. They are preoccupied with their work and have little or no relationship with God through Jesus Christ. When Jesus told Peter to cast down his net for a catch, he was reluctant to do so because Peter had toiled all day but had nothing. When he did at the command of Jesus, Peter took the biggest catch of his life. Peter became the rock upon which the Lord built His church. When we spend quality time with the Lord, He will reward us because our Lord is the rewarder of those who iligently seek Him (Hebrews 11:6). Investment in the word of God brings in everlasting prosperity. If we take care of the tree (the Lord) and His branches (all people), the Lord will bless us forever. If He cares for the birds of the air (sparrows), He will take care of us if we take care of His church and sheep. James challenges us about the perfect gifts of God.

> ***"All perfect and good gifts (either riches or wealth) are from above and cometh down from the Father of lights, with whom is no variableness, neither shadow of turning"***
>
> ***James 1:17***

To receive a perfect gift from the Father, we must put Him first by having a perfect relationship with Him. Many people are working very hard all the time, but they are still poor because God is not first on their priority list. If God is first in everything we do, He will shower His perfect and eternal riches and wealth on us.

2. Money, Money, and Money: Does money really matter in the kingdom of God?

Jesus taught about money more than any other topic in the Bible because it is one of the most spiritual traps on earth. Money has always been a constant source of anxiety for many who love it. It is a source of anxiety for both the poor and the rich. There is an element in money called greed that gives us insatiable desires. King Solomon discussed the danger of greed in Ecclesiastes.

> ***"He that loveth silver shall not be satisfied with silver, nor he loveth abundance with increase: this is also vanity"***
>
> ***Ecclesiastes 5:10***

There is something in money that urges man to grab and grab forever. The abnormal increases in wealth accumulation set you for all kinds of evil. Jesus has nothing against money. He is not condemning possessions or ownership of assets or even enjoying what God has provided you in life. Jesus is not telling you to renounce earthly treasures and join a convent or monastery. He is looking for disciples who will use their wealth wisely to advance the Kingdom of God *(Proverbs 6:9-11)*. Neither is Jesus suggesting that Christians should not aspire to greatness or excellence. He is not forbidding owning a house, a car, or good clothes, or having a good GPA, a degree, a bank account, or some other assets. Jesus is not telling us, don't ever save any money, and just spend every penny we get. Financial responsibility is a lesson of the Bible.

The book of proverbs has many texts to say about responsible financial lifestyles, such as giving, saving, wise investing, and leaving an inheritance to children's children Proverbs 1:19; 6:6-8; 10:4; 12:11; 13:11; 14:23; and 24:33-34). While building wealth is encouraged in Proverbs, doing so from a heart of greed is not. Trusting in God for our sustenance is a good step toward remembering where the money comes from, which should lead to humility rather than a belief in our own abilities to grow wealth in our own stren. Apostle Paul admonishes parents to leave generational wealth for their grandchildren.

> ***"Behold, the third time I am ready to come to you, and I will not be burdensome to you: for I seek not yours, but you: for the children ought not to lay up for the parents, but the parents for the children"***
>
> ***2 Corinthians 12:14***

Jesus and his disciples lived off of the financial generosity of those who had accumulated some wealth. We can use some of the money and all kinds of wealth to get through life and provide for our families, but the lesson is that don't see these things for more than what they are. Don't build your life around these things because most people get consumed by them. The focus of their life is about accumulating cars, homes, collections, and all forms of investments, and they are all going to be lost. Jesus is warning us against the improper values that we place on these treasures. It is through that which so ties us to the world that we risk losing eternal life. It is our affection for these things that give treasures undue values. The choices we make today may result in eternal treasures in heaven.

However, earthly treasures will not guarantee us heavenly treasures. Most hypocrites in the church and the world do what they do hope, for the reward of being noticed by people here on this earth. Today, there are many millionaires and philanthropists who give to institutions or other organizations for immediate reward in the form of huge ovation in public, naming a building after, and other kinds of recognition instead of the church, missions, and the needy. They like the praise of men more than the praise of God *(John 12:43).* It is to be noted that the world is not a good place to invest your treasures forever. Worldly investments are temporal and perishable because you can lose all of them when you die, or experience natural disasters. Holy Spirit is telling us to invest our wealth in heaven where returns are guaranteed and 100 percent. In the stock market, investors are not guaranteed a 100 percent return because, in many cases, they get negative and lower returns over time. It is smart business to trade something temporary for something eternal. Yet, it is the sad truth that many Christians are hardly investing in the church, missionaries abroad, evangelism, and the needy. Don't waste your life on things that are all going to melt away one day. It is a smart move that you don't leave this life and go to heaven empty-handed. Invest your life, money, and time in saving up treasures in heaven that can never be taken away.

To better understand the truth about choosing investments in the kingdom of God or the world, we need to separate this truth into parts. First, we will visit Paul's first letter to Timothy:

> ***"For the love of money is the root of all evil: which while some coveted after, they have erred from the faith and pierced themselves through with many sorrows. But thou, O man of God, flee these things; and follow after righteousness. godliness, faith, love, patience, meekness"***

> ***1 Timothy 6:10-11***

Money itself is not the root of all evil, but the love of money is. As soon as it becomes a source of our security, even if it is only a source of security, we will end up in trouble. God's kingdom is the only safe place to use our money if we hope for any eternal rewards. Again, Paul warns us not to be arrogant or trust in uncertain wealth but rather to put our hope in God by generously giving and sharing with the saints *(1 Timothy 6: 17-19).* Whatever treasures we store up in heaven will be waiting for us when we make it in heaven. The way to avoid treasuring up treasures upon the earth is to treasure up treasures in heaven by developing a Christ-like character, maintaining a personal relationship with Christ through personal devotions and soul witnessing.

The church is not innocent in church business and the race to make merchandise of the word of God as well as the push for prosperity over spirituality. In the late 20th century, it was an exposure of television evangelists' extravagant lifestyles. Today, there are cults who charge exorbitant fees for tuition to attain a higher level of spirituality or prosperity preachers who promise personal prosperity to those who will send in "seed money". These pastors, teachers, prophets have turned the truth of the word of God because lies and negative news sell and thrive than truthful news. The whole world is treading on negative news because people like lies more than the truth. These false preachers are feeding the congregation what they want to hear. Lies run around the world, dressed as the truth, and society is very happy because the world has no desire to know the naked truth (***Jean-Leon Gerome, 1896***)

What are the dangers of perverting the truth about prosperity?

- False teachers are significantly more than the real, and they deviate from the truth *(1 Timothy 6:3).* We need sound teaching that comes from Christ and promotes godliness.

- False teachers tend to divide the church for their own advantage. The false teachers are characterized as proud and knowing nothing as well as being obsessed with controversies and quarrels over words.

- False teachers are money lovers and think that godliness is a means of gain. The truth is that godliness with contentment is great gain.

> ***"But godliness with contentment is great gain.***
> ***For we brought nothing into this world, and it***
> ***is certain we can carry nothing out"***
>
> *1 Timothy 6: 6-7*

Behind the desire of false teachers is greed. Greed is a trap for the rich, the poor, and everyone in between. In general, we waste financial resources because we buy more than we can afford since our wants are more than our needs. So much is going to waste instead of going into the Lord's kingdom. The characteristics of those who love money are:

- They are more concerned with making more money by any means.

- They never have enough of it. They will chase money till death.

- They tend to flaunt it. The pride of life becomes their slogan *(1 John 2:16).*

- They resent giving any away. They become like the young rich ruler who turned away from Jesus when he was asked to share his wealth with the poor, and

They often sin to get it. They cheat people, the system, and in most primitive communities, they use human sacrifices.

Apostle Paul reminds us, for some rich people, their pursuit of wealth has turned many from the faith. They have also suffered many things in their pursuit of wealth. Many have wealth but have no peace of mind. As a child of God, we are commanded by the Lord to flee from the things that characterize the lives of false teachers He is also to flee from any teaching that robs Christ of his glory. He is also to flee from those who think that godliness is a means to financial gain. The Christian life is the pursuit (Follow) of spiritual virtues such as righteousness-godliness, faith-love, and patience-gentleness. Also, the Christian life is riddled with spiritual warfare so fight a good fight of faith. Finally, a Christian must fasten on or lay hold on eternal life to which you were called and have confessed the good confession in the presence of many witnesses *(1 Timothy 6:12)*.

3. Get real with the Word of God

Let us remember that all that we pack, gather, and save in the form of houses, cars, assets, clothes, jewelry, and more will be left behind on earth after we breathe our last. It is, therefore, a smart choice to invest more in the kingdom of God. We are not telling you not to save money, get a home or a car because we can use some of these things to get through life and to provide for our families. The heavenly advice is that do not build your life around these things. For most people, the focus of their life is about accumulating cars, houses, collections, and investments, but they are going to lose them all.

The Lord is not on earth with us, so we carry out all his missions by helping the needy, supporting the missionaries, and helping to reach the ends of the world (global evangelism). There is joy in helping to meet the needs of the poor everywhere. By doing for our friends and others, we are doing it for the Lord. We should not expect rewards when we give because we are building our treasures in heaven.

God owns everything we have. We have to trust him in all we undertake. If we do not invest in His kingdom, He can take everything away from us. We do not have to listen and look to the world but be content with what we have. We do not have to get greedy in whatever enterprise we undertake. Do not let money and material possessions compromise your Christian faith.

God has a spirit of excellence, so we will have to work by inviting God into our business. Success is not a sudden flight that is why we need a divine connection from God. God plus Business is a success.

It cost John the Baptist his life when he invested in the kingdom of God by preaching repentance. It also cost Jesus Christ his life when he established the spiritual church in the kingdom of God by preaching the good news. Similarly, it cost all the apostles their lives by crucifixion and related deaths, by torture. What has it cost you being a Christian? Today the devil is in almost all churches so there is virtually no persecution going on. The devil will not tackle you if you run the same path with him. Today's teaching and preaching is not hitting the devil hard as they did in the first-century church. Satan is inside the church and taking many Christians to hell. Many false teachers and prophets in churches all over the world are wolves in sheep clothing who are teaching and preaching doctrines of devil and man by making godliness a gain.

This is a terrible and grievous thing in the modern Church. It should cause us the fear of God to withdraw ourselves from those who are perverting the ways of truth. It should break our hearts and move us to pray and labor to bring our brothers and sisters out of this end-time deception. Remember, end-time deception is deepening as the Lord's coming draws near. We dare not compromise our stance against this "gospel" of greed when the Scriptures are so clear against it. If we compromise, then, we too, are in danger of being deceived, for if we fail to receive and act upon the light that we have been given, even what we have been given may be taken away.

4. Final Thoughts

The Apostle Paul calls the false teachings of prosperity preachers "Perverse disputings" of men of corrupt minds, and destitute of the truth, supposing that gain is godliness: from such withdraw yourself." *(1 Tim. 6:5).*

Again, Paul says that these men think that the godlier you are, the more monetary gain you are going to get. They say that if you really have faith and are godly, you will be financially prosperous. But this is perverse and corrupt teaching. And the Scripture commands us to withdraw ourselves from such preachers! Have you withdrawn yourself from these false teachers? Or are you continually listening to their teaching and soaking up their ungodly ramblings and adulterous perverting of Scripture? Will you obey the Word of God and "come out from among them"

> *"Wherefore come out from among them, and be ye separate, saith the Lord, and touch not the unclean thing; and I will receive you."*
>
> *(2 Cor. 6:17)*

Furthermore, Paul admonishes us that, "But godliness with contentment is great gain. For we brought nothing into this world, and it is certain we can carry nothing out. And having food and raiment let us be therewith content. But they that will be rich fall into temptation and a snare, and into many foolish and hurtful lusts, which drown men in destruction and perdition." *(1 Tim. 6: 6-9)*.

We are called to be content with our disposition, even if we have nothing more than clothes on our backs and the necessary food to eat. But those who desire to be rich, fall hard from the faith into temptation and many foolish lusts and are drowned in destruction. It continues to say that they merely will be, or desire, to be rich. Yet these prosperity preachers openly admit that they want more, that they desire to have more abundant earthly possessions and financial security. Truly, by their own admission, by their own words, they are destitute of the truth. False teachers deceive men, and in turn, are deceived by Satan and his demons. They are like rich fools.

> ***"And I will say to my soul, Soul, thou hast much goods laid up for many years: take thine ease, eat, drink, and be merry. But God said unto him, Thou fool, this night thy soul shall be required of thee, then whose shall those things be, which thou hast provided? So is he that layeth up treasure for himself, and is not rich toward God"***
>
> ***(Luke 12:19-21)***

Similarly, Peter warns us about false teachers in the last days: "But there were false prophets also among the people, even as there shall be false teachers among you, who privily shall bring in damnable heresies, even denying the Lord that bought them, and bring upon themselves swift destruction. And many shall follow their pernicious ways; by reason of whom, the way of truth shall be evil spoken of. And through covetousness shall they with feigned words make merchandise of you: whose judgment now of a long time lingereth not, and their damnation slumbereth not" *(2 Pet. 2:1-3).*

Let's break down what Peter is saying and look at it one statement at a time, comparing it with these prosperity preachers that have infiltrated our churches and ministries.

Peter says that there were false prophets in times past and shall be false teachers among us. So by this statement, we need to take heed and recognize that there are false teachers among us. Peter clearly said there would be, so that must mean that there is. Therefore, we need to understand that the Scripture promises us that they are among us and warns us that we need to identify them so as not to be deceived by their cunning craftiness. Paul warns us to be extra vigilant in the end times in order not to lose our salvation.

"See then that ye walk circumspectly, not as fools, but as wise. Redeeming the time, because the days are evil"

Ephesians 5:15-16

Peter says that they secretly bring in damnable heresies, even denying the Lord. We have already seen that this "gospel" of greed and prosperity is a damnable heresy since it causes people to covet earthly things in their hearts and provokes the jealousy of God, and the Scripture says that the sin of covetousness is a damnable sin that will exclude one from the Kingdom of God. This heresy of a covetous "gospel" has secretly crept into the Church because it comes disguised as something good, cloaked with biblical terminology and extracted from quoting Scriptures out of context. It is secret because it's a hidden thing from the eyes of most that it is wrong. Most don't recognize it as being heresy and it secretly deceives them. These false teachers deny the Lord not by plainly saying, "I deny the Lord" –that would be too obvious. They deny the Lord by denying His true teachings, and by teaching things that are contrary to what He taught. In denying His truth, they are denying him with their teachings and practices. Even though they claim to serve Him with their lips, their hearts are far from Him. They claim to love the Lord with their words, but they deny Him in their hearts by loving the things of this world *(Matthew 15:8).*

> *"Who changed the truth of God into a lie, and worshipped and served the creature more than the creator, who is blessed forever. Amen"*
>
> *Romans 1:25*

Peter says that many will follow their pernicious ways and because of them, people will speak evil of the way of truth. Are we not seeing this fulfilled before our very eyes? There are not a few who follow these prosperity preachers, but many —multitudes upon multitudes of people. And because of their constant ramblings that say that we should be rich or financially prosperous, people who are not Christians blaspheme Christianity and say, "They just want money".

Peter says that these false teachers, in their covetousness, will exploit us and make merchandise of us with their deceptive words. This is exactly what these prosperity preachers are doing. They are motivated by covetousness, they are motivated by the desire to have more money and in this motive, they give appeal after appeal to their audiences to give them more donations. They preach entire sermons on why we should give money to their ministries. They see the people in their congregations as mere merchandise, and they speak great speeches on why we need to give them more money! They create gimmick after gimmick to try to motivate people to give to them. It's the height of deception!

Finally, Peter says that their damnation does not slumber. If those who are using the things of God to get monetary gain for themselves and are exploiting the people of God with clever speeches and deceptive words, if they don't confess their sin, repent, and get cleansed by the blood of Jesus from all covetousness, then they will surely be swallowed up by damnation from the pit from whence their false doctrines come. The Apostle Peter is not playing games with false doctrine and heresy and speaks in unmistakable and harsh language against these things because he knew that they would deceive so many sincere people. False teachers abound in poor nations of Africa, Asia, and Latin America and continue to exploit the church and the congregation.

The prophet Isaiah said, "His watchmen are blind: they are all ignorant, they are all dumb dogs, they cannot bark; sleeping, lying down, and loving to slumber. Yea, they are greedy dogs which can never have enough, and they are shepherds that cannot understand: they all look to their own way, every one for his gain, from his quarter." **(Isa.56:10-11).**

This is the state of these churches where these prosperity preachers are overseeing. They are blind and ignorant; they cannot see any danger approaching, and they can't recognize the subtle tricks of the enemy to deceive people. These preachers are dumb dogs that cannot bark; they don't give any warning of danger approaching and they don't preach against sin and warn people to flee the wrath to come. They rarely preach on the Judgment or on hell. Instead, they are in a spiritual slumber and aren't prepared themselves for the coming of the Lord. They love to slumber. They love their ease and prosperity and luxurious living. They are greedy dogs that can never have enough as they are constantly exploiting people to give more and more money into their ministries, accumulating more treasure on earth, and increasing their luxurious lifestyles more abundantly as time goes on. They are shepherds who can't understand the true things of God and are constantly looking not for the well-being of the souls of the flocks they are preaching to but are constantly looking for their own selfish gain.

This is a terrible and grievous thing in the modern Church. It should cause us the fear of God to withdraw ourselves from those who are perverting the ways of truth. It should break our hearts and move us to pray and labor to bring our brothers and sisters out of this end-time deception. Remember, end-time deception is deepening as the Lord's coming draws near. We dare not compromise our stance against this "gospel" of greed when the Scriptures are so clearly against it. If we compromise, then we, too, are in danger of being deceived, for if we fail to receive and act upon the light that we have been given, even what we have been given may be taken away. *(Luke. 8:18).*

It cost John the Baptist his life when he invested in the kingdom of God by preaching repentance. It also cost Jesus Christ his life when he established the spiritual church in the kingdom of God by preaching the good news. Similarly, it cost all the apostles their lives by crucifixion and related deaths by torture. What has it cost you by being a Christian? Today the devil is in almost all churches, so there is virtually no persecution going on. The devil will not tackle you if you run the same path with him. Today's teaching and preaching is not hitting the devil hard as it did in the first-century church. Satan is inside the church and taking many Christians to hell. Many false teachers and prophets in churches all over the world are wolves in sheep clothing that are teaching and preaching doctrines of devil and man by making godliness again.

5. Let's Pray

Heavenly Father, thank you for your son Jesus Christ, who died and resurrected for me, ***Insert your name about here.*** Give me your Holy Spirit to live in me forever and thus bless me with eternal life. Let your Holy Spirit testify through me and speak the truth through me. Lord Jesus, help me to have a generous attitude of giving to the church, evangelist, and the needy. Through generous giving, I ***insert your name about here,*** prove that God is first in my life, and I honor him ***(Deut.14:23. Prov.3:9).*** Give me a perfect and unselfish Holy love so that I can lay down all worldly ambitions. Lord, I submerge my will into yours. Take my thoughts away from making greedy money or finding selfish business opportunities. Take my eyes away from looking on vain worldly appearances, which deceive and mislead me.

Let power change hands in my finances, in the name of Jesus. Let favor from men and women rush wealth to my doors. I destroy every clock and timetable of poverty in Jesus' name. O Lord, transfer the wealth of Laban to my Jacob. I take over the wealth of the sinner in the name of Jesus. O Lord, plant in me, **insert my name about here,** a reference point of divine blessings. Every effect of strange money affecting my prosperity be neutralized in the name of Jesus. Every arrow of wickedness fired against my prosperity, be disgraced, in the name of Jesus. I reject caged finances in the name of Jesus. I ***insert your name about here,*** reject every spirit of debt and bankruptcy in my life be paralyzed now, in the name of Jesus. I will not take my eyes off the Lord Jesus in the name of Jesus. In the end, Lord let me know that godliness with contentment is a great gain. Help and lead me away from the worldly richness that has led many into foolish and hurtful lusts. Most of all, move me from prosperity preachers and prophets who are lying and tricking people on the truth about worldly richness.

Father, let me not lay up for myself treasures upon earth, where moth and rust doth corrupt, and where thieves break through and steal. But let me lay up for myself ***insert your name about here,*** treasures in heaven, where neither moth nor thieves abound. God, without you, I will easily succumb to materialism, become a prisoner of my debt, and be unable to experience the joy of generous giving.

Lord, please remind me to give 10 percent of my income to the needy and the work of God. Lord Jesus, help me ***[insert your name about here]*** to learn more about God's love and care for me when I am willing to invest more of myself in God and invest more of my life in God's missions in the world. I do, hope, however, that as I invest more and more in the kingdom of God and grow to put less stock in finding happiness in the things of this world and more stock in the relationships acquired through the riches of God's grace.

Open my spiritual eyes to see that heaven is my ultimate home and the world is my temporary home. Grant me, ***insert your name about here*** inner spiritual strength to resist temptations and to control my mind. Your Word never dies, and it remains the same till now ***(Hebrews 13:8).*** May God grant me wisdom and make me strong. Let me ***insert***

your name about here, abide in you forever and ever in the name of Jesus.

Lord, help me to have faith that will make me live, save, and spend for the kingdom of God in Jesus' name. Lord, don't let me leave this life and go to heaven empty-handed in Jesus' name. Help me **_insert your name about here_** to invest my life, money, and time in saving up treasures in heaven that can never be taken away. Lord, let me do good all the time, be rich in good works, ready to give, willing to share and lay hold on eternal life in the name of Jesus.

Jesus Christ defeated the whole kingdom of darkness and won an overwhelming victory by disarming principalities and powers at the cross. Jesus Christ is the victor. He is the mighty conqueror. Jesus triumphed over all his foes, and he has given me complete victory over every foe in my life. This includes a victory over Satan, the demons, and the whole kingdom of darkness, as well as victory over all works of darkness, including witches and wizards. Therefore, Satan, demons, witches, and warlocks, you have absolutely no power and no authority over me *(Luke 10:19)*. Lord of glory; let your kingdom come through the power of the Holy Spirit and the glory of God. I *[insert your name about here]* seal this prayer with the precious blood of the Great Shepherd of the sheep and thanksgiving. In Jesus' name, I pray, Amen.